POP MUSIC THEORY

HARMONY, FORM, AND COMPOSITION

Second Edition

POP MUSIC THEORY

HARMONY, FORM, AND COMPOSITION

DR. MICHAEL JOHNSON
BERKLEE COLLEGE OF MUSIC

CINEMASONIQUE MUSIC
MONOMYTH MEDIA
BOSTON, MASSACHUSETTS 02148

Library of Congress Cataloging-in-Publication Data
Johnson, Michael J.
        Pop Music Theory-2nd ed.

ISBN: 978-0-578-03539-0

Art Director / Cover Design: Amberlee Chaussee
Cover Illustration: Svetlin Rusev
Executive Editor: Andrea Johnson
Printer / Binder: Lulu Press
Typeface: 12 Arial Black

To purchase additional copies please visit:

http://www.lulu.com/content/1183612

To learn more about Dr. Michael Johnson visit:

purevolume.com/michaljjohnson and www.myspace.com/michaeljohnson0664

This book is dedicated to my lovely wife Andrea for her love and support over the years.

About the Author

Dr. Michael Johnson is Associate Professor at Berklee College of Music where he lectures in Songwriting and Arranging in the Contemporary Writing and Production department. He draws upon seventeen years of teaching experience, seven of which he served as Director of Commercial Music at Greenville College. There he mentored many students who went on to be signed by major record labels, including members of Augustana (SONY/BMG), whose song "Boston" went on to top the Billboard charts.

He is a nationally recognized ASCAP songwriter whose independent rock releases have been featured in films such as "Night Becomes Day" and "Samsara." Summit Records houses one of his finest jazz compositions, "His Song" and as an arranger he has nationally published the work entitled "Celebrate".

In the music industry, he has performed for twenty-five years as a guitarist and vocalist along side such "heavies" as Jon Secada (EMI), Lari White (RCA), Dawnn Lewis (A Different World), Take Six, Bob Dorough and Kevin Nealon (Saturday Night Live). In the studio he performed soundtracks for Royal Caribbean Cruise Lines, The Orange Bowl Half-Time Show, CPP Belwin (Warner Bros.), and The Record Plant in Miami, Florida.

Dr. Johnson recently authored two university-level textbooks entitled "Pop Music Theory" and "Jazz Vocal Improvisation" which are setting new standards in the music education market by delivering online texts, podcasts, video instructional blogs, PowerPoint lectures and e-exam materials for music professors. He currently resides in Boston, Massachusetts as a member of the Independent Film Society of Boston. Examples of his work can be found at purevolume.com/michaeljjohnson, and www.myspace.com/michaeljohnson0664

We've included new features that you'll love.

- **Key Terms** help students reinforce chapter vocabulary.

- **Self Check Questions** help students review their understanding of the core concepts presented before moving on to study further materials.

- **Tips for Composers** help students focus on key strategies to expand their critical thinking and listening skills.

- **Building Your Musical Skills** help students apply chapter concepts and build skills through writing exercises in the supplementary workbook.

Teaching Tools
For Professors

- **Professor's Edition** contains three-holed punched textbook that includes fully explained In-Class Activities, Homework Assignments, Teaching Tips, Quick Quizzes, Lecture and Chapter Outlines, Supplemental Reading Recommendations, Case Studies and Handouts.

- **Test Item File** has been updated to include a variety of questions for every chapter. Each question is fully referenced to corresponding learning objective, chapter heading, page references and difficulty level.

- **Professor's Resource Center** at www.monomythmedia.net instructors can access a variety of print, digital and presentation resources available with this text in a downloadable format. Registration is simple, giving you immediate access to new titles and new editions. The following supplements are available to adopting instructors.
    - Online E-Textbook: developed for professors and students who need access 24/7
    - E-Exams and Printed Test Item File
    - Study Guides
    - Instructional Videos
    - Blogs from the Author
    - Powerpoint Slides
    - Teaching Outlines
    - Course Syllabus
    - Teaching Calendar
    - Chapter Reviews in downloadable MP3 or Podcast format
        - Key Terms: Audio flashcards that review key concepts and term
        - Practice Test: lets students know if they need to keep studying
    - Internet Bookmark links for additional reading and study
    - Recommended Listening Examples
    - Learning Module for Students: Each chapter offers an online 5-question pretest, a summary for review, an online learning activity, and a 10-question post-test
        - Requires an access code, which can be obtained from the publisher.

Acknowledgments

We would like to thank the following friends for their encouragement and support in the review and compilation of this text.

Dr. Walter Barr
Metropolitan Community College

Amberlee Chaussee
Aubergine Designs

Sandie Chaussee
Jaguar Woman Sounds

Don Gorder, Esq.
Berklee College of Music

Ken and Shirley Johnson

John Kellogg, Esq.
Berklee College of Music

Larry Lapin
University of Miami

Gary Lindsay
University of Miami

Ron Miller
University of Miami

Dr. Matt Nichol
Berklee College of Music

Whit Sidner
University of Miami

TABLE OF CONTENTS

POP MUSIC THEORY

HARMONY, FORM, AND COMPOSITION

INTRODUCTION

The study of popular music theory and composition is a relatively new field. It is, however, a timely development when one considers that it has been more than 45 years since "Rock Around the Clock" appeared on the Billboard charts, more than 70 years since the beginnings of Tin Pan Alley, and close to 100 years since Scott Joplin began publishing his ragtime compositions.

Those who have already taken classical or traditional theory must first understand this: Some of the standard rules will not apply. One obvious example is the use of parallel fifths, which is commonly used in rock music. Additionally, some popular music is "modal" music, or music that is not necessarily based on the standard major and minor key structures found in tonal classical music. Put in the simplest terms, modal music usually lacks the typical tonic-subdominant-dominant relationships that usually serve to establish a *tonal center*. This is not to say that the listener does not recognize a tonal center; rather, it is established in different ways than the customary I-IV-V7-I chord progression. Many standard jazz compositions consist solely of a series of ii-V7-I progressions. However, these are used in such a way that the tonal center seems to change every two to four measures.

Throughout the course, the following areas will be discussed as they relate to popular music:

- e **Chord Construction and Nomenclature** - The way in which chords are constructed and used in pop music, and the use of chord symbols.
- e **Scales** - The role of scales in pop music harmony, especially Chord-Scale Theory, or the use of scales to construct chords.
- e **Pop Music Arranging** - Arranging for a small ensemble, and writing lead-sheet arrangements.
- e **Pop Music Composition** - Different styles and composers will be studied, as well as pop music compositional techniques.
- e **Ear Training** - The student will learn to recognize chord qualities and chord progressions, as well as the use of scales for improvisation and "ad libbing". They will also learn to transcribe music from recordings.
- e **Keyboard** - The primary goal is the ability to play chord changes, which is useful for self-accompaniment as well as composition.

Why Should I Care About Pop Music Theory?

It is important and beneficial knowledge for those in almost every area in popular music. Anyone involved in the music industry should be able to compose. Copyright ownership is an excellent source of income, and one never knows when an opportunity will arise to write a song or collaborate on a song for another artist. The following are some of the ways music theory knowledge relates to different segments of the entertainment industry:

- **Performers** - A good performer, whether a singer or instrumentalist, should be able to write out a *Chart* (written arrangement) for a song in the appropriate key. In addition, everyone knows that a musician who also composes will be better equipped to make a living. There are plenty of band members in the world who are not composers, thus never earning a penny until the record company recoups their advance.
- **Recording Engineers** - A recording engineer who understands music will get more gigs! It's also true that many clients will ask the engineer for production advice, and the ability to give such advice will also increase your demand.
- **Producers** - Most modern producers are also songwriters and arrangers.
- **Songwriters** – No further explanation required.
- **Music Business Professionals** - A deeper understanding of what you are listening to could never hurt, no matter what aspect of the industry you are in. If you are in the A&R field, you may find yourself participating in production decisions at times. In addition, you may find that your access to the major labels gives you an opportunity to moonlight as a freelance songwriter!

Just as musical knowledge is important for those in the music industry, it is also important to understand the business side, even for composers and performers. Creative types should also be familiar with the technological aspects of the industry as well. The key to success in the music industry today is versatility. Once you have learned your craft in your own particular area, try to acquire skills and knowledge in as many other related fields as possible. This will make you more marketable in the industry, and you may not even have to flip burgers to support your music habit!

What Is Popular Music?

The term "Popular Music" can be a bit confusing, as it is used in many different ways. When musicologists use the term, they are generally referring to any style of music outside of the realm of "classical" or "art" music. Thus, Popular Music includes Jazz, Rock, Blues, R&B, Hip-Hop, Contemporary Christian Music, Country & Western, and even Southern Gospel and Black Gospel. Of course, the term is generally used to describe music that originated in The United States, and it is often referred to as "American Popular Music." Paradoxically, The Beatles, one of Rock's most influential groups, came from England.

However, today's popular music evolved from the cultural melting pot of early America, so the term "American Popular Music" is essentially correct. In fact, much of it is the direct result of the merging of European and African musical traditions that could have only occurred in America. Reggae, Calypso, Salsa, and other Latin American, Afro-Caribbean and Afro-Cuban styles, which involved in much the same way, are often labeled as "World Music." Yet, they share many common traits with American Popular Music. Furthermore, many of these styles have become a part of American musical culture in recent years.

Popular Music writers and "Rock Critics" such as those who write for magazines like "Rolling Stone" and "Spin," use the term "Pop Music" in a different way. The term is often interchangeable with "Top 40," a term that describes music which is played on popular, or Top 40 radio stations. In this context, Pop, Rock, Hip-Hop, and R&B are distinct musical styles. For example, the Billboard Top 40 charts are often referred to as the "Pop Charts." Additionally, critics often use the term to describe music which is "catchy," "melodic" or well crafted. Thus, a Heavy Metal or Grunge band may be described as having a "pop sensibility," meaning they compose "catchy" or "singable" melodies.

The term "Classical Music" can also be very confusing. Musicologists use the term to describe the art music composed from 1750-1825. However, the term in American popular culture describes any music that lies outside the popular mainstream. Indeed, many laymen assume that music performed solely by a symphony orchestra is classical music. However, many modern symphony orchestras regularly perform "pops" concerts. Furthermore, the film music of composers such as John Williams, while performed by symphony orchestras, has achieved great popularity. It is also interesting to note that most jazz styles beginning with the Be-Bop period in the 1940's have appealed to an increasingly selective and intellectual audience. As it has always been assumed that popular music appeals to the masses and classical or art music appeals to a select intellectual audience, this would indicate that most modern jazz could be described as a form of American classical music.

For the purposes of this text, the term "pop music" will include Top 40, CCM, Rock, R&B, Hip-Hop, and other similar styles. Indeed, for theoretical purposes, Country & Western, Southern Gospel and Black Gospel could be included in this description. Jazz, however, often follows theoretical rules that differ from other styles of popular music as well as classical. When this is the case, a distinction is made between usage in Jazz and Pop. Furthermore, the reader should assume term "classical" to include all art or "serious" music written from the Medieval period to the present. The reader may have noted that Jazz Fusion, Acid Jazz and Smooth Jazz, as well as Art, Progressive and Jazz Rock fall into a bit of a "gray area." Most Jazz Fusion evolved from Modal Jazz, which follows most of the same theoretical rules as pop music. The other styles, while occasionally borrowing ideas and sounds from classical and jazz, usually derive theoretical constructs from pop music.

The term "Western Music" often describes music derived from European musical traditions. Do not confuse this term with "Country and Western" music. Western music in this sense includes most American and European classical, jazz and popular music. The division of the octave into twelve tones, as well as our musical notation system, is all part of Western musical tradition. This term differentiates our music from that of other cultures, most notably the East (China, Japan, India, etc.)

Tips for Composers

- **Listen constantly** – Some pop artists claim they never listen to the radio, reasoning that they don't want their ideas tainted by the music of others. Most of them are currently residing in the "where are they now?" file!
- **Listen actively** - with an analytical ear
- **Listen to what is current in your particular genre.**
- **Listen to as many different styles as possible** - In this day and age, more and more composers are borrowing elements from other musical styles, even ethnic and world music.
- **Transcribe** – This doesn't necessarily mean you always have to transcribe to paper; simply learning to play songs helps to expand your musical vocabulary.
- **Maintain your performance chops** – Even if you consider yourself more of a composer than a performer, it is a good idea to look for opportunities to perform once in a while. As with listening, it is also a good idea to perform as many different styles as possible. Many of the best composers are also performers. Composers often end up performing their own music because they cannot find performers who are willing or able to perform it.
- **Always be open to inspiration, but don't rely on it** – Composers often go through periods of inspiration followed by periods of "writer's block". Song ideas can come through reading, meditation, or tinkering on the piano or guitar.
- **Carry a small tape or digital recorder with you** – You never know when you might have an inspiration. It may come to you in the car, or in the middle of the night.
- **Schedule time every day for composing** – Even if it is an hour each day, having a steady time set aside for composing is a good idea. You may also wish to begin each composing period with a time of quiet meditation (and you may want to check out the book "The Artist's Way", which contains many good ideas for this type of daily regimen.) There may be days when you accomplish nothing, but in general, you will find a daily schedule to be fruitful.
- **Don't be afraid to tinker or revise**– Very few of us can get it perfect the first time. Revision is part of inspiration – that's why we have intellect. On the other hand, be careful not to second-guess yourself too much. At some point, you have to move on to other songs!
- **Try not to be thin-skinned** – Our compositions are our "babies." Don't be devastated if your friends don't like your songs. Be open to criticism, but remember that any critique is just one person's opinion. Furthermore, don't be disappointed if *you* are not happy with your songs. Sometimes it's a good idea to distance yourself from a song for a few weeks, then listen again with "fresh ears." Above all, don't be overly self-critical; it's just music, not brain surgery! And one more word about writer's block: It happens to the best of them. Don't give up on your writing just because you go through a dry spell.

Versatility as a composer is also very important, so learn to compose in as many different styles as possible. Only a handful of composers can make a living solely on writing pop songs and pitching them to others. Many artists today are also composers, and they are not interested in recording other people's songs. However, a composer can pursue other freelance opportunities:

- **Composing for film and television** – Be aware that many film scoring projects will involve writing for orchestra. If you wish to pursue this, you should study orchestration, or at least read some orchestration books. TV projects, however, especially for local television, can often be achieved with a good MIDI setup.
- **Composing for industrial videos** – Many large corporations have in-house video production facilities, and specialty video production companies produce industrial videos. Many of them use pre-recorded music that they license. However, with a bit of networking, you might be able to get some work scoring their videos.
- **Composing for multimedia, video games, and the Internet** – This is a relatively new and growing market. Again, they will often license pre-recorded music. A composer must sometimes be a salesperson in order to get gigs.
- **Commercial Jingles** – Still a very lucrative avenue for composers. Commercial jingle composers often produce the recording in their home studios. Contacting ad agencies and radio stations in your area is probably the best method. Be careful when negotiating contracts for this type of work. A local jingle is usually produced on a buyout, or one-time payment, so be sure that you are paid adequately for your time. Regional and national jingles, however, can often lead to residual royalty payments, so you may need to accept a smaller up-front fee.
- **Arranging** – There are a variety of arranging and orchestration jobs out there, ranging from small ensembles to large orchestras. Some churches with large music programs will hire arrangers and composers to write for their ensembles.
- **Copying** – Years ago, before computer music notation, record labels, recording studios, film scoring composers, and movie studios hired professional copyists to write out instrumental parts for orchestras and bands. This type of opportunity is rare these days. However, a composer who is adept at using a notation program such as Finale or Sibelius can still find gigs entering a handwritten score into the program and generating parts.

Most employers must hear a demo recording or "demo reel" before they hire you. One of the most important tools for a modern composer is a home MIDI or audio recording studio and notation software. Pro Tools LE, Digital Performer, Logic Audio, Cakewalk Pro Audio, and Cubase are all excellent programs. A good demo can be produced with one of these programs, a synthesizer/workstation, and a CD burner.

Review: Basic Theoretical Concepts

It is assumed that those using this text have taken at least one year of traditional music theory. At the very least, the reader should know how to read music. If this is not the case, there are many excellent books on basic theory available. This book does include several review sections, however, and most readers who posses basic musical knowledge should be able to understand all of the concepts discussed.

Intervals

An *interval* is the distance between two notes. It is important to learn the relationship between the visual appearance, construction, and sound of an interval. The smallest interval in the Western harmonic system is the half step. It is also the basic building block for all intervals. If you look at middle C on the piano keyboard, an ascending half step is the distance to the next adjacent note: D♭ (or C♯,) and a descending half step is the distance between C and B. A half step is also the interval between two adjacent frets on one string of the guitar.

Another term used to describe a particular kind of half step is "Minor Second." The next highest interval is the whole step, which is equal to two half steps. The whole step is also called the "Major Second." There are two types of intervals, the "Major/Minor" intervals, which are the seconds, thirds, sixths and sevenths, and the "Perfect" intervals, the fourths, fifths and octaves. Table A lists the intervals in ascending order, from smallest to largest, culminating with the octave. Example A displays all of the intervals to the octave in ascending and descending format.

Table A. Number of Half Steps in Each Interval

No. of half steps	Interval name
1 half step	Minor 2nd
2 half steps	Major 2nd
3 half steps	Minor 3rd
4 half steps	Major 3rd
5 half steps	Perfect 4th
6 half steps	Tritone (Augmented 4th, Diminished 5th)
7 half steps	Perfect 5th
8 half steps	Minor 6th (Augmented 5th)
9 half steps	Major 6th
10 half steps	Minor 7th
11 half steps	Major 7th
12 half steps	Perfect Octave

Example A Intervals

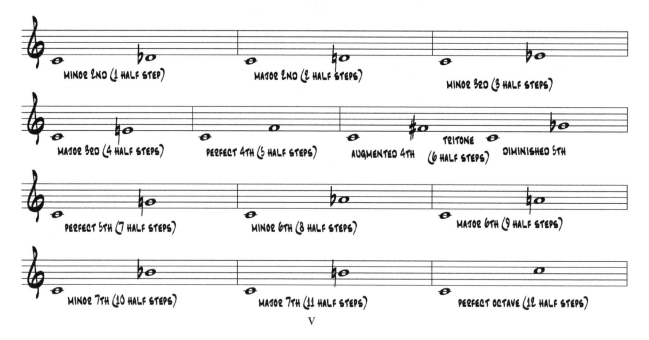

v

The Major Scale and Key Signatures

The *Major Scale* is the basis of traditional Western harmony. It is a system of dividing the octave into a series of whole steps and half steps. The major scale is an *Asymmetrical Scale*, in that it has an odd number of notes (seven notes, not including the octave,) and an unequal number of whole steps and half steps. The whole steps and half steps of the major scale are in a prearranged order. Example B illustrates the order of whole steps and half steps as found in the C major scale.

Example B The Order of Whole Steps and Half Steps in the Major Scale

The root, or first note, of a major scale is determined by the *Key Signature*. The key signature determines the number of sharps or flats, if any, needed to achieve the correct order of whole steps and half steps from the root of the scale. Sharps and flats are also arranged in a certain order. Flats are arranged in the order BEADGCF, and sharps are arranged in the order FCGDAEB. The *Circle Of Fifths* has long been used to conveniently organize the major keys in an easily understandable fashion. Figure A illustrates the Circle of Fifths.

It is important that the student memorize the order of the sharps and flats as well as the circle of fifths. Complete knowledge of all of the major keys is essential to any well-rounded musician.

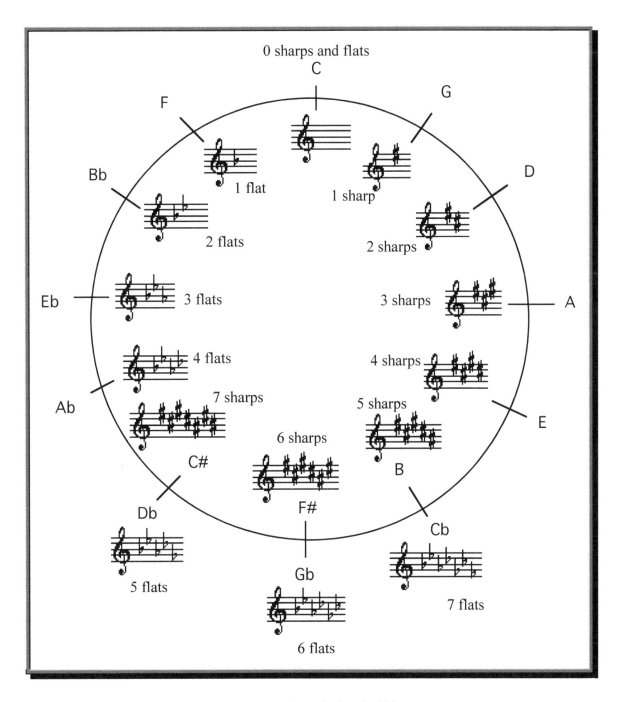

Figure A. The Circle of Fifths

Tonality

Tonality is the organization of musical material around a central note, usually called the *Tonic* or *Tonal Center*. In the major scale, the tonal center is the root or first note of the scale. *Tonal Music* is music that is organized around a tonal center. Most classical music until the mid- to late-19th century was tonal. In the 20th century, however, composers of "classical" music abandoned traditional ideas of tonality. Modern classical composers often use all twelve of the notes available in the Western tonal system, a practice called *chromaticism*. The word chromaticism refers to the use of the *Chromatic Scale*, a scale consisting of all twelve notes found in the octave. Example C illustrates the chromatic scale starting on C, notated in flats and sharps. Note that there is a half step between each note of the scale.

Example C The Chromatic Scale

Chromaticism can also refer to the use of notes not found in the scale or mode on which an otherwise tonal composition is based. The use of chromaticism in a composition does not necessarily mean that it lacks tonality. Listeners will often perceive a tonal center in chromatic music, even if the tonality seems to be constantly shifting. A composition in which the tonal center is constantly shifting or changing may also be referred to as chromatic in nature. *Atonal Music* is music in which the composer makes an effort to avoid any perception of tonality.

Although chromaticism is often found in popular music, atonality is rare. It should also be noted that many popular songs are not based on a major scale. In most of these cases, however, there is still a sense of tonality. The root of the scale is usually perceived as the tonal center.

1

TRIADS

Triads are the basic building blocks of harmony. *Harmony* is achieved when two or more notes are sounded simultaneously. A triad is a group of three notes sounded simultaneously. The five types of triads are major, minor, diminished, augmented and suspended. A *chord* is a group of two or more notes sounded simultaneously; thus, triads are also the basic building blocks of chords, and a triad can also be called a chord. The type of triad used determines the *Chord Quality*. In other words, a major chord consists of a major triad; a diminished chord consists of a diminished triad, and so on. Chord qualities will be discussed further in the section on chord nomenclature. A *Chord Progression* is a series of chords that make up all or part of a musical composition. This term is used because the chords "progress" from one to the next.

A triad is usually made up of two intervals of a third, stacked on top of each other. Table 1.2 lists the thirds contained in each type of triad, and Example 1.2 illustrates them in the form of musical notation. Note the inclusion of the "suspended" triad, in which the natural 3rd of the chord is replaced by the 2nd or the 4th. In classical music the suspended fourth chord is usually expected to resolve to a major chord, with the movement of the fourth degree down to the third. However, in pop music the suspended fourth chord, usually called a "sus4," is not necessarily expected to resolve. In more recent times, the suspended second, or "sus2" chord has also seen frequent use. The sus2 is built on a principle similar to the sus4. The natural 3rd is lowered by a whole-step, resulting in a "3rd" a major 2nd above the root.

The three notes of a triad are referred to as the root, third and fifth, in ascending order. It is also important to note the interval between the root and fifth of the triad. In the major, minor, sus2 and sus4 triads, the interval between the root and fifth is a perfect fifth. In the diminished triad, the interval between the root and fifth is a diminished fifth, and the interval between root and fifth of an augmented triad is an augmented fifth. Thus, the diminished and augmented triads derive their names from the interval between the root and fifth.

Table 1.1. Intervals Contained in Triads

Triad	Interval from Root to 3rd	Interval from 3rd to 5th	Interval from Root to 5th
Major	Major 3rd	Minor 3rd	Perfect 5th
Minor	Minor 3rd	Major 3rd	Perfect 5th
Diminished	Minor 3rd	Minor 3rd	Diminished 5th(Tritone)
Augmented	Major 3rd	Major 3rd	Augmented 5th
Sus4	Perfect 4th	Major 2nd	Perfect 5th
Sus2	Major 2nd	Perfect 4th	Perfect 5th

Example 1.1. Triads

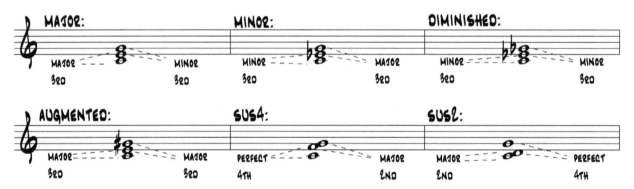

Triads can also be inverted, meaning that the bottom note is not the root of the triad. This can sometimes be confusing to the eyes as well as the ears when one is trying to ascertain the chord or triad type. A triad is in *First Inversion* when the bottom note is the third of the triad. A triad is in *Second Inversion* when the bottom note is the fifth of the triad. In all cases except with regard to the suspended triad, first or second inversion are easily identified on paper, in that the intervals will be that of a third and a fourth, rather than two thirds. It is interesting to note, however, that the augmented triad sounds the same in first and second inversion as it does in root position. This is because the interval between the fifth of the chord and the octave above the root is a diminished fourth, which is the same as a major third. Example 1.2 illustrates the different inversions found with each type of triad.

Example 1.2 Triads and Inversions

While pop harmony also includes more complex chords than simple triads, triads are the basis for all chords, and it is important to be familiar with them.

Keyboard Assignment 1.1: Learn to play the triads and inversions pictured in Example 1.2, in all keys, in the right hand.
Ear-Training Assignment 1.1: Identify the chord quality of each triad.

Chord Nomenclature for Triads

The term *Chord Nomenclature* refers to the chord's label. In other words, the proper use of *Chord Symbols*, the form of shorthand used to indicate the chords used in a composition. A standard chord symbol applied to a triad will consist of the following two components: a.) The pitch level from which the chord is built, and b.) The chord quality, or type of triad, indicated by a *Chord Suffix*. A Chord Suffix is a label following the pitch name of the chord, used to describe the chord quality. Chord suffixes may also include added 7^{th}s and extensions, as discussed in later chapters. Table 1.2 illustrates the standard use of chord symbols for triads built from the pitch "C".

Table 1.2. The Use of Chord Symbols for Triads

Pitch Level	Chord Quality	Chord Suffix	Chord Symbol
C	Major	(None required)	C
C	Minor	Minor, min, m, -	Cminor, Cmin, Cm, C⁻
C	Diminished	Diminished, dim, °	Cdiminished, Cdim, C°
C	Augmented	Augmented, aug, +	Caugmented, Caug, C+
C	Suspended 4th	Sus4, sus	Csus4, Csus
C	Suspended 2nd	Sus2	Csus2

Note the number of possibilities for some of the chord symbols. Any of these are acceptable, and in fact there is no standard method. It is best to pick one type of chord symbol and be consistent. Also note that a C major chord is simply notated as "C". There is no need to add the suffix "Major".

Example 1.3. Closed Position Triad Piano Voicings

Review 2: Chord Function and Cadences

In traditional (classical) tonal musical practice, chords fulfill a certain function in major and minor keys. Composers adhered to this tradition for hundreds of years until near the end of the 19th century. Example 1.4 illustrates the chords built on the scale degrees of the major and minor scale:

Example 1.4. Chords in Major and Minor Keys

The Roman numerals used to denote the scale degrees are also used to indicate the type of chord. Uppercase Roman numerals indicate a chord with a major 3rd, while lowercase numerals indicate a chord with a minor 3rd. In addition, the plus (+) sign indicates an augmented triad, and the circle (°) a diminished triad. It is important to remember that these are conventions used in the analysis of traditional classical music. However, there are some similar conventions used in pop music. For instance, some composers will use an uppercase "m" (CM) to indicate a major chord, and a lowercase "m" to indicate a minor chord. This can be confusing at times, especially in handwritten notation, where it is often difficult to distinguish an uppercase letter from a lowercase one.

One further point should be stressed with regard to Roman numerals. In traditional music theory, there are certain chord suffixes used to denote chord inversions. These are not applicable to pop chord symbols. It is best to disregard classical chord suffixes from this point on.

Cadences are rules that govern chord progressions in traditional tonal music. Cadences are also used in the composition of melodies. A cadence is used to bring music to a point of rest, or conclusion. The most obvious point of rest in a composition is at the end. However, a chord progression will usually consist of many intervening cadences as well.

The *Authentic* cadence produces the most dramatic sense of finality in traditional music. This cadence consists of the V (or V7) chord followed by the I chord. The downward root movement of a perfect 5th is a very strong point of rest, and it lends the perception of finality even in more chromatic music. The *Plagal* cadence, IV to I, tends to sound less conclusive, yet it is still used quite often. For instance, the words "Amen" at the end of a hymn are sung to a plagal cadence.

The *Half* cadence lends an "unfinished" sound to a musical phrase. A half cadence usually ends on a IV or V chord. A section of a song that is repeated twice will usually end with a half cadence the first time through, in order to lead back to the I chord at the beginning of the repeated section.

The *Deceptive* cadence consists of a V chord followed by a chord other than I, most often VI. It is called deceptive because the listener expects the V chord to lead to the I chord. Example 1.5 illustrates examples of each of these cadences:

Example 1.5. Cadences

In common tonal practice, the half and deceptive cadences are typically interior cadences, used within the structure of a song or section of a song. Although they may also be used at the end of a section, they are rarely used to conclude a composition. Authentic and plagal cadences, however, can serve as interior cadences as well as at the end of a song.

Popular musicians, however, often make an effort to rebel against conventional rules. While many pop songs follow these rules, one can find just as many examples of compositions that do not.

Use of Triads in Popular Music

Major Triads

Triads, though very simple types of chords, are extensively used in all forms of popular music, with the exception of some jazz styles. In the first several decades of Rock & Roll, it was not uncommon to hear songs consisting entirely of major triads. Example 1.6 illustrates a common 16-bar chord progression found in 1950's Rock & Roll (in songs such as "Jailhouse Rock" and "Rockin' Robin.")

Example 1.6. Standard 16-bar Rock and Roll Chord Progression

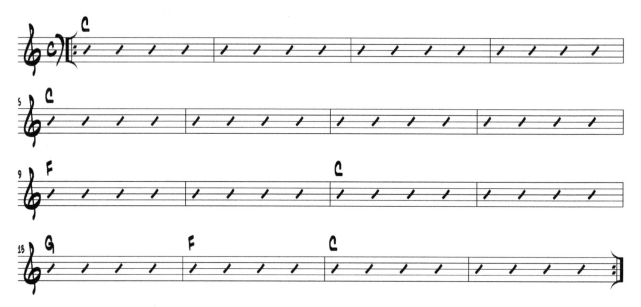

Minor, Diminished and Augmented Triads

Minor, diminished and augmented triads are rarely used exclusively in a pop composition. Minor and diminished triads frequently are utilized just as they are in tonal classical music. Minor triads typically serve as ii, iii, and vi chords in major keys, and i chords in minor keys. Diminished triads usually serve a dominant function. Augmented triads are also commonly used in a dominant function, or to create tension. Sus2 triads often serve as substitutions for major triads, creating a more "open" sound than a major chord. Finally, sus4 triads may fulfill the function of any major triad as well, and are especially strong as dominant chords. While it is not uncommon for the 4th to resolve down to the natural 3rd, it is also acceptable if the chord does not resolve.

Open 5th chords

While technically not triads, open 5th chords are often used in hard rock and heavy metal styles. The chord includes only two pitches, the root and 5th, as illustrated in example 1.7.

Example 1.7. Open 5th Chord.

The most common chord symbol for this chord is C5, as illustrated. However, other possibilities are C (no 3rd) or C (omit 3rd). In hard rock and heavy metal, these types of chords are usually played on the guitar, and they are also known as *Power Chords*. Open 5th chords are typically used in place of major or minor triads, especially in hard rock styles.

Written Assignment 1.1

Introduction to the Nashville Numbering System

The *Nashville Numbering System* is a system used for the notation of chord progressions in Nashville, Tennessee. Variations of this technique are used in other areas of the U.S. and other musical styles, but it is most closely associated with Nashville and Country music. The system is similar to the Roman numeral system used in the analysis of classical music. However, Arabic numbers (1,2,3, etc.) are used instead.

Example 1.8 illustrates the chords built on the C major scale, utilizing Nashville numbers in place of Roman numerals:

Example 1.8. The Chords in C Major with Nashville Numbers

Note that the nomenclature is similar to that of pop chord symbols. A minus (-) sign (or a lowercase "m") indicates a minor triad. The circle (°) indicates a diminished triad. In addition, the plus (+) sign is used for augmented triads. A number with no suffix indicates a major triad.

Obviously, the Nashville system is based in traditional tonality, specifically the major scale. The key of the song is established by the composer/arranger, and the remaining chords are numbered accordingly. If a chord that is not usually found in the key is used, the number is preceded by a "♭" or "♯" (according to the chord usage.) Flats are probably more common in this case. For example, if a song is in the key of C major, but includes a B♭ major chord, that chord will be labeled as "♭7".

Composers and arrangers often write arrangements using the Nashville system. These are called *Nashville Number Charts* (or Nashville Charts or Number Charts.) Nashville number charts do not include traditional notation. In fact, one does not even need to know how to read music in order to use it. However, it does require knowledge of the function of major keys.

A Nashville chart will usually contain traditional measure lines, although this is not always the case. A typical Nashville number chart, using measure lines, is illustrated in Example 1.8:

Example 1.9. 16-bar Rock and Roll Progression, Nashville Number Chart

||: 1 | ' | ' | ' | ' | ' | ' | ' |
| 4 | ' | 1 | ' | 5 | 4 | 1 | ' :||

Note the use of the double bar at the beginning and end, as well as the repeat sign. The slash with a dot on either side is a measure repeat symbol, indicating that the chord played in the previous measure is repeated. Figure 1.1 illustrates a measure repeat symbol:

Figure 1.1. Measure Repeat Symbol

Nashville number charts can be created on a computer using a word-processing program. Measure repeat symbols can be found in the fonts that come with most music notation software. The symbols above were created using Finale® fonts. However, if no such software is available, a percent (%) sign is adequate. Furthermore, measure repeat signs are not required. The chord number can also be repeated in each measure.

Another common format for Nashville notation charts is the Box Chart. In a box chart, boxes are used to represent each measure. Example 1.10 illustrates a typical box chart:

Example 1.10. Nashville Number System Box Chart

1	'	'	'
'	'	'	'
4	'	1	'
5	4	1	'

Repeat signs can also theoretically be used in a box chart, although these are more problematic in terms of formatting, especially when created with a word processor.

A third type of Nashville number chart does not include lines indicating each measure. This would typically be used only in cases where only one chord is played in each measure. A line is used at the beginning and end of each section in the form, and measure repeat symbols are not used (Example 1.11.)

Example 1.11. Nashville Number Chart Without Measure Lines

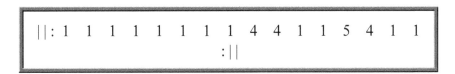

||: 1 1 1 1 1 1 1 1 4 4 1 1 5 4 1 1
:||

The type of chart illustrated in Example 1.11 is perhaps more difficult to follow than the other two examples, in the opinion of the author. Above all, a chart must be easy to read.

The Nashville system is quite flexible. Any chord suffix can be used with the numbers. Additional musical symbols, such as rests and fermatas, can be used as well. There are also methods for notating 1st and 2nd endings and held chords. The composer or arranger will usually indicate the major sections of a song, such as the verse and chorus. All of these will be discussed in later chapters.

The main advantage of using Nashville notation is that a song can be played in any key. This is perhaps why it has been used so successfully in Nashville. For instance, if the singer in a recording session feels that the key is to high, a new chart does not have to be written. The band simply chooses a new key. The system is also useful for guitarists using a capo.

From this point on in the text, Nashville numbers will be used for analysis in most cases. However, conventional chord symbols will be used as well. However, the reader should be aware that in some segments of the jazz and commercial industry, especially in educational circles, Roman numerals are still utilized to explain these concepts.

Checklist of Assignments for Chapter 1

✓ **Keyboard Assignment 1.1:** Learn to play the triads and inversions pictured in Example 1.2, in all keys, in the right hand.

✓ **Ear-Training Assignment 1.1:** Identify the chord quality of each type of triad.

✓ **Keyboard Assignment 1.2:** Learn to play the "closed position" piano voicings pictured in Example 1.3, in all keys. Note that each utilizes the three inversions in the right hand, while the left hand plays only the root. These are labeled "closed position" because the right hand plays triadic chords, with the notes as close together as possible, and the left plays the root. This is standard practice in pop music.

✓ **Written Assignment 1.1**

2

SIMPLE POP CHORD PROGRESSIONS

In the 1950's, early Rock and Roll shared many common traits with Country and Western. This is to be expected, as Rock and Roll blended elements of Country and Western and early Rhythm and Blues. Early Rhythm and Blues, in turn, evolved from the Blues. The standard chord progressions used in all of these styles were typical diatonic progressions, following the tonic-subdominant-dominant-tonic form. At times the 4 chord and 5 chord were used interchangeably. In Example 2.1, a 4 chord in measures 10 and 14 precedes the 1 chord in measures 11 and 15. The 5 chord only appears in measure 13, near the end of the 16-bar phrase.

Example 2.1. Standard 16-bar Rock and Roll Chord Progression

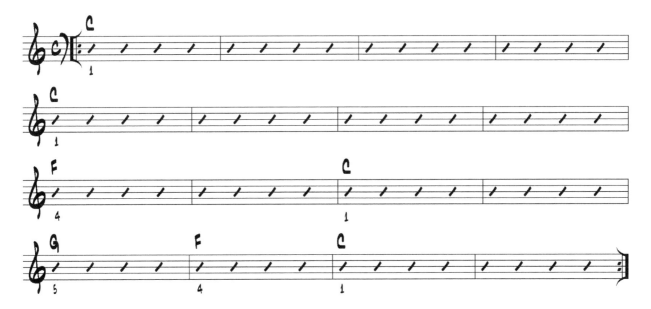

This chord progression is sometimes referred to as a 1-4-5 Rock and Roll progression.

Many chord progressions were borrowed from earlier musical styles as well, such as the 1-6m-4-5 and 1-6m-2m-5 progressions borrowed from big band song forms such as "Rhythm Changes," as well as the 12-bar Blues.

The 12-bar Blues Progression in Rock and Roll

The 12-bar blues was used extensively in the 1950's. The blues is one of the oldest purely American musical styles, and indeed all of our modern popular music styles are believed to have evolved from the blues. This includes Jazz, Rock, Gospel, R&B (which actually stands for Rhythm & Blues,) and even Country & Western. The most easily distinguishable characteristic of the blues is a 12-measure form. Many different varieties of blues have existed over the years, including an 8-bar and 16-bar form, but the standard 12-bar form has remained the most popular. Example 2.2 illustrates the standard rock & roll blues progression.

Example 2.2. Standard Rock & Roll Blues Progression

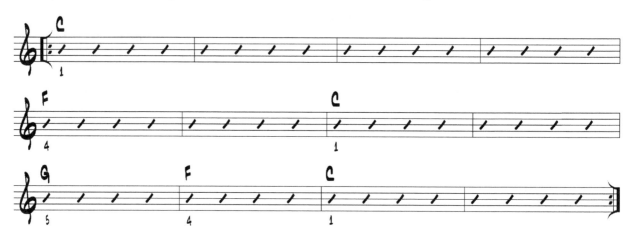

It is perhaps easier to understand the blues using the Nashville number format, as illustrated in Example 2.3:

Example 2.3: The Blues, Nashville Numbers

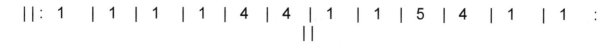

||: 1 | 1 | 1 | 1 | 4 | 4 | 1 | 1 | 5 | 4 | 1 | 1 :||

Written Assignment 2.1: Write out the Standard Rock and Roll Blues Progression in any key.

Chord Substitutions

Refer again to the standard 16-bar Rock and Roll chord progression, illustrated in Example 2.1. Note that the tonic, subdominant and dominant chords are used exclusively. However, the chord which precedes the 1 chord (measures 10-11 and 14-15) is the 4 chord, rather than the 5.

Many composers soon grew bored with the static harmony in this early chord progression, and they began utilizing *Chord Substitutions*, a technique in which a composer substitutes one chord for another. Many times this meant simply rearranging the order of the 1, 4 and 5 chords, but often they would add one or more chords that technically did not fit in the key. One example of this is illustrated in Example 1.5.

Example 2.4. Standard Rock and Roll Chord Progression with Chord Substitution

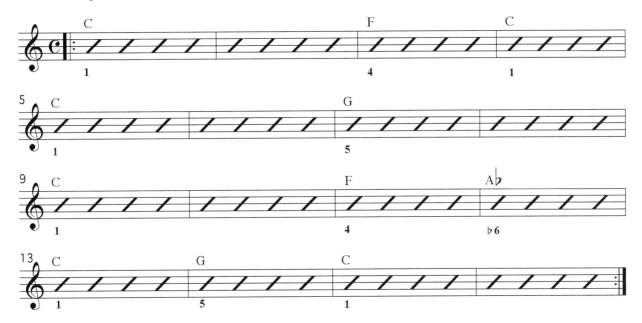

Note the chord in measure 12, A♭ Major, not normally found in the key of C. ♭7 and ♭6 chords are commonly used in pop music. In traditional theoretical terms, one might suggest that both chords are borrowed from the natural (Aeolian) minor scale or key. In other words, the chord substitution is borrowed from another key, in this case, C minor.

1-6m-4-5 and 1-6m-2m-5 Progressions

Many Doo-wop hits of the 1950's contained 1-6m-4-5 progressions, such as *Earth Angel, In The Still of The Night*, and *Blue Moon*. Indeed, that progression and its cousin the 1-6m-2m-5 progression have been in use in nearly all pop music styles since the early 20th century. Example 2.5 illustrates these two progressions in the key of C:

Example 2.5. 1-6m-4-5 and 1-6m-2m-5 Progressions

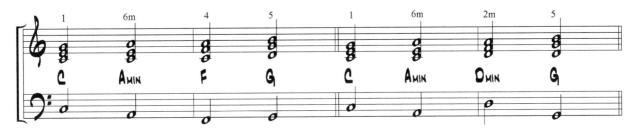

Another similar chord progression is the minor version, which we will call the 1m-♭6-4-5 progression. Less frequently used, but still worth mentioning, is the 1m-♭6-2°-5 progression. You may recall that in traditional theory, the 2 chord is diminished in minor keys, and it is usually the same in pop music. Example 2.6 illustrates the minor 1m-♭6-4m-5 and 1m-♭6-2°-5 progressions.

Example 2.6. Minor 1m-♭6-4m-5 and 1m-♭6-2°-5 Progressions

When discussing the above progressions, composers and musicians will usually use the generic terms "1-6-2-5" and "1-6-4-5," referring to both the minor and major versions, and leaving out the chord suffixes. In fact, in many jazz texts, as well as some other pop theory texts, Roman numerals will be used. This will be the case with some of the other standard progressions discussed in later chapters as well.

Additional Pop Chord Progressions

There are a number of other rock chord progressions made up solely of triads. Some of them are rather simple and diatonic in nature, while others contain some chords not normally found in the key. Rather than explain these in detail, some examples are listed in Tables 2.1 and 2.2 below.

Table 2.1. Diatonic Progressions

Nashville Numbers	Examples (Key of C)	Nashville Numbers	Examples (Key of C)
1-1sus	C-Csus	1-1+-4-5	C-C+-F-G
1sus-1	Csus-C	1-1+-4-4m	C-C+-F-Fmin
1-5sus	C-Gsus	1-4-5-4	C-F-G-F
1-4	C-F	1-5-4-5	C-G-F-G
1-6m	C-Amin	1-5-6m-4	C-G-Amin-F
1m-♭6	Cmin-A♭	1-5-6m-5	C-G-Amin-G
1-1-4-5	C-C-F-G	1-5-6m-3m	C-G-Amin-Emin
1-4-5-1	C-F-G-C	1-2m-3m-4	C-Dmin-Emin-F
1-4-5sus-5	C-F-Gsus-G	1-3m-4-5	C-Emin-F-G
1m-4m-5sus-5	Cmin-Fmin-Gsus-G	1m-♭3-4m-5	Cmin-E♭ –Fmin-G
1-4-6m-5	C-F-Amin-G	1m-♭7-♭6- ♭7	Cmin-B♭-A♭- B♭

Table 2.2. Non-Diatonic Progressions

Nashville Numbers	Examples (Key of C)
1-♭7	C-B♭
1-♭6	C-A♭
1-♭5	C-G♭
1-♭7-4	C-B♭-F
1-♭7-♭6-5	C-B♭-A♭-G
1-♭7-♭6-♭7	C-B♭-A♭-B♭
1-5-6-5	C-G-A-G
1-♭7-♭3-4	C-B♭-E♭-F
1-♭3-4-5	C-E♭-F-G
1-♭3-4-♭3	C-E♭-F-E♭
1-4-♭7-4	C-F-B♭-F
1-4-5-3	C-F-G-E
1sus-1-♭7sus-♭7-♭6sus-♭6-5sus-5	Csus-C-B♭sus-B♭-A♭sus-A♭-Gsus-G

Do not assume that the above list is comprehensive. There are many other useful progressions available using simple triads. There are also a number of chord progressions that do not begin with a 1 chord, but we will touch on those later. Note that many of the progressions do not end with a 5 chord. To fans of modern popular music, often a 4 chord, or even a ♭7 or ♭3, are equally effective in leading to the 1 chord.

Almost all of the above progressions are interior cadences, usually repeated a number of times in the course of a song.

Written Assignment 2.2: List three pop songs that utilize diatonic chord progressions, and three pop songs that utilize non-diatonic chord progressions, and indicate the progression used.

Turnaround Progressions

A *Turnaround* is a chord progression used at the end of phrase or section of a song to get to the next phrase or section. As such, the cadences are also usually interior cadences, as they are meant to lead back to the 1 chord. Typical turnarounds are 1-4-1-5, 1-6m-4-5,1-6m-2m-5, 2m-5, or even just a 5 chord. Turnarounds usually end with the 5 chord, except in cases where the song does not begin with a 1 chord. In these cases, the final chord of the turnaround usually acts as a *Secondary Dominant*, leading to the chord that begins the next section. A Secondary Dominant is a 5 chord borrowed from the key of the chord that follows it. For instance, if a song in the key of C begins with the 2m chord (Dmin,) the secondary dominant would be borrowed from the key of D. The 5 chord in the key of D is A. Therefore, the turnaround would end with an A chord. A typical turnaround progression in this case would be C-F-C-A, or 1-4-1-6.

Keyboard Assignment 2.1: Choose two pop songs from a fake book that consist solely of triads, and learn to play the chord changes.
Written Assignment 2.3: Analyze the two pop songs utilized in Keyboard Assignment 2.1 using Nashville numbers.
Written Assignment 2.4: Compose a 16-measure chord progression, using only triads and/or open 5th chords, with at least one chord per measure. Use chord symbols, rather than Nashville numbers.

Checklist of Assignments for Chapter 2

- ✓ **Written Assignment 2.1:** Write out the Standard Rock and Roll Blues Progression in any key.
- ✓ **Written Assignment 2.2:** List three pop songs that utilize diatonic chord progressions, and three pop songs that utilize non-diatonic chord progressions, and indicate the progression used.
- ✓ **Keyboard Assignment 2.1:** Choose two pop songs from a fake book that consist solely of triads, and learn to play the chord changes.
- ✓ **Written Assignment 2.3:** Analyze the two pop songs utilized in Keyboard Assignment 2.1 using Nashville numbers.
- ✓ **Written Assignment 2.4:** Compose a 16-measure chord progression, using only triads and/or open 5th chords, with at least one chord per measure. Use chord symbols, rather than Nashville numbers.

3

FORM, RHYTHMIC NOTATION, AND LEAD SHEETS

The ultimate goal of this chapter is to instruct the reader in the creation of *Lead Sheet* arrangements. A lead sheet is a bare-bones arrangement of a song consisting of melody, lyrics, and chord symbols. Lead sheets are designed to fit a large amount of information about an arrangement into a very small space. They should be easy to read, and between 1-3 pages in length. However, before we explore lead sheets, the subjects of form and rhythmic notation must be discussed.

Analysis of Form in Pop Music

The most common method for musical analysis is the use of the letters of the alphabet. This method is effective with almost all styles of music. However, it is important to first understand the different components of modern pop songs.

The Major Sections of a Pop Song

The terms *verse*, *pre-chorus*, *bridge*, and *chorus* are most commonly used to describe the different major sections of modern pop songs. In addition, *instrumental break* and *solo* are used to describe sections of a song that do not include a vocal melody. In most pop compositions, each major section will be the same length, usually at least 16 measures, although 8 or 12 measure sections are occasionally found.

Identification of the different sections and their function in the song can sometimes be difficult. The lyrics and melody are often the best way to make such an analysis. The chorus is sometimes the easiest section to spot, as it generally will consist of the same melody and lyrics every time. In addition, the chorus often contains the title of the song. The message of the song, or the main point the lyricist is attempting to convey, will be featured prominently in the chorus.

A pre-chorus usually consists of a repeated melody every time, and sometimes even the same set of lyrics. The function of a pre-chorus is to musically and lyrically lead in to the chorus, and will usually occur before each chorus. The pre-chorus is sometimes shorter than the other major sections.

Pre-choruses are often confused with bridges. However, a bridge usually happens only once in a pop composition. The typical function of a bridge is to provide a musical contrast and further clarify the lyrical message. Often a bridge will seem to modulate to another key for at least a few measures, eventually leading to the original key or modulating to a new key for the next chorus. The bridge is usually placed near the end of the song, and often helps to build the musical and emotional intensity. Some of the most well crafted pop songs are constructed similar to a short story, with the climax occurring at the last chorus or choruses. The bridge, then, often occurs immediately before the climax of the song, building up to the climax.

The verse of a song can also be fairly easy to identify, as it usually occurs first, after the introduction. A verse is usually made up of the same melody, but with different lyrics each time. The first task is to determine how long a verse is, for it is not uncommon for two or more verses to occur before any other section of the song. The melody or lyrics may help in determining each new verse, as well as a simple comparison with the length of the chorus.

Instrumental breaks and solo sections often consist of the same chord progression as the verse, pre-chorus, bridge or chorus. However, sometimes a new chord progression is composed for the instrumental section of the song. A solo section can also serve the same function as a bridge, and in these cases it occurs in place of a bridge. The most common type of solo section in pop music is the guitar solo, although keyboard and saxophone solos are popular as well.

Not all pop compositions contain a bridge and pre-chorus. However, almost all pop songs consist of verses and a chorus. The sequential order of the major sections can differ greatly from song to song. However, there are some common configurations, as illustrated in Figure 9.1:

---

verse, pre-chorus, chorus, bridge:
verse – verse - pre-chorus – chorus – verse - pre-chorus – chorus – bridge – chorus

verse, pre-chorus, chorus:
verse – verse – pre-chorus – chorus – verse – pre-chorus – chorus – chorus

verse, chorus, bridge:
verse – verse – chorus – verse – chorus – bridge – chorus – chorus

verse, chorus:
verse – verse – chorus – verse – verse – chorus – chorus

Figure 3.1. Common Pop Song Forms

The Glue That Holds a Pop Song Together

Modern pop compositions usually include an *introduction* or *intro*, *interludes* or *transitions*, and a *coda* or *outro*. Introductions/intros are typically 4 or 8 measures long, and are often made up of the chord progression found in the verse or chorus. Occasionally, however, an intro may be composed of completely different musical material from the rest of the song, such as a riff.

Interludes/transitions are sometimes identical to the intro, especially if the intro includes a riff. The purpose of such a section is to provide a transition between a chorus and verse, or between two verses. Transitions are rarely found before or after a bridge or pre-chorus. The coda/outro can be made up of a variety of elements. It may be a reiteration of the intro, or an instrumental repeat of the verse or chorus with a fade-out at the end. A coda may also consist of a "tag," repeating the last four measures of the chorus. A repeat of the chorus at the end of a song cannot really be considered an outro unless it is shorter or significantly different than the other choruses. Even a fade-out of the chorus may not necessarily constitute an outro or coda, although this is open to debate.

Note that the two terms given above for each of these three types of sections are interchangeable. For instance, the words interlude and transition both describe the same kind of thing, and either term can be used. However, a song can include several transitions made up of different musical material, one between verses and one between chorus and verse. Not all pop compositions contain all three types of sections. In fact, a few songs contain none of them. Figure 9.2 illustrates a common pop song with all of the major song sections plus an intro, transitions, and a coda:

> intro – verse – transition – verse – pre-chorus – chorus – transition –
> verse – pre-chorus – chorus – bridge – chorus - coda

Figure 3.2. Common Pop Song With Intro, Transitions, and Coda

Analysis of Pop Song Form

As mentioned above, upper-case letters of the alphabet are the simplest tools for pop song analysis. In practice, the letters are used sequentially to indicate the major sections of a song when they first appear, without regard to their function in the composition. In other words, B does not necessarily indicate a bridge, and C does not necessarily indicate a chorus; Rather, B indicates the second major section to appear, and C indicates the third.

It is usually best if intros, transitions and codas are treated as separate entities. If a song contains two different transitions, they can be listed as "transition 1" and "transition 2." Abbreviated section titles are acceptable. Solo or instrumental sections should be assigned a separate letter if they contain new musical material, and the word solo or instrumental should be indicated in parentheses. If a solo is played over the changes of a verse or chorus, the corresponding letter can be used, and the word solo or instrumental in parentheses. Figure 3.3 illustrates the analysis of a common pop song form, with the analysis in bold type:

(Intro	A	Trans.	A	B	C	Trans.
intro –	verse –	transition –	verse –	pre-chorus –	chorus –	transition –

A	A (solo)	B	C	D	C	Coda)
Verse –	verse (guitar solo) –	pre-chorus	– chorus –	bridge –	chorus –	coda

Figure 3.3. Analysis of a Typical Pop Song

Bear in mind that the melody and lyrics are often the best gauge as to whether a section is a verse or chorus. Some pop compositions contain only one chord progression repeated over and over again, and the only way to differentiate the chorus from the verse is the melody and/or lyrics.

Written Assignment 3.1: Analyze the form of two pop songs from different genres or eras.

A Few Standard Rules for Rhythmic Notation

There are several rules to be followed when notating rhythms. These are standard rules that apply to all styles of music. These conventions exist so that the performer may easily read notated rhythms.

Quarter- and Eighth-note Rhythms

When notating rhythms in 4/4 time involving a mixture of quarter- and 8th-notes, there is one golden rule: the third beat of the measure must be easily identifiable. Think of the area between beats two and three as a line that cannot be crossed without using a tie. The following examples illustrate incorrect and correct notation of these types of rhythms:

Example 3.1. 8th–Quarter–Quarter–Quarter–8th Rhythm

Incorrect Notation: **Correct Notation:**

(Note: The incorrect rhythmic notation in Example 3.1 is not absolutely forbidden, as it is fairly easy to read, and it has been utilized in some published works. It is suggested, however, that the notation style labeled as correct be used whenever possible.)

Example 3.2. Dotted Quarter–Quarter–Dotted Quarter Rhythm

Incorrect Notation: **Correct Notation:**

Example 3.3. Dotted Quarter–Dotted Quarter–Quarter Rhythm

Incorrect Notation: **Correct Notation:**

Note that, in each case, 8ᵗʰ notes are tied between beats two and three, in order to clearly delineate where beat three is.

There is, however, one exception to the rule. A quarter-note, half-note, quarter-note rhythm need not be tied between beats two and three, as illustrated in Example 3.4:

Example 3.4. Half Note on Beat Two

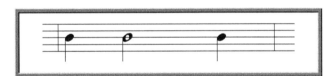

When dealing with other time signatures, rhythmic notation must be modified accordingly. As a rule of thumb, even-numbered time signatures should be treated in a similar fashion. Furthermore, in time signatures with more than 4 beats per measure, there should be a division between every two to three beats, depending on the rhythmic feel or "groove." For instance, 6/8, 9/8 and 12/8 are usually subdivided every three beats, and the pulse is usually felt every three eighth notes. Thus, 6/8 is felt in two, 9/8 in three, and 12/8 in four, as illustrated in Example 3.5:

Example 3.5: 6/8, 9/8 and 12/8

Rhythms in 6/8 should be notated so that the line between beats three and four are clearly indicated. Similarly, the dividing lines in 12/8 time should be between beats three and four, six and seven, and nine and ten (Example 3.6.)

Example 3.6. Rhythmic divisions for 6/8, 9/8 and 12/8

In non-standard time signatures with more than 4 beats per measure, the listener often discerns subdivisions of two or three beats within the measure. It is up to the composer/arranger to determine which subdivisions will best support the desired groove. For instance, 5/4 may be subdivided into three beats followed by two beats, or two beats followed by three beats. Similarly, 7/4 is often subdivided by three, two and two or two, two and three. The rhythms should be notated to reflect the intended rhythmic subdivision.

In 2/4 and 3/4 time, there is obviously no rhythmic subdivision, and the composer/arranger must make a judgment as to how a rhythm is most easily read.

8th- and 16th-Note Rhythms

When notating rhythms consisting of a mixture of 8th and 16th notes, the division between each beat must be clear. The following examples illustrate incorrect and correct methods of notating 8th- and 16th -note rhythms:

Example 3.7. 16th–Quarter–Quarter–Quarter–Dotted 8th Rhythm

Incorrect Notation: **Correct Notation:**

Example 3.8. 16th Followed by Seven 8th Notes Followed by 16th Rhythm

Incorrect Notation: **Correct Notation:**

Beaming of 8th and 16th Notes

In 2/4 and 4/4 time, 8th notes should be beamed together by the beat (Example 3.9.)

Example 3.9. 8th Notes Beamed Together by the Beat

If the first two beats of a measure contain all 8th notes, these four can be beamed together (Example 3.10.)

Example 3.10. Four 8th Notes

The dividing line between beats two and three must be observed, however, when notating 8th notes (Example 3.11.)

Example 3.11. 8th Notes and the Dividing Line Between Beats 2 and 3

In 3/4 time, each beat is beamed separately (Example 3.12.) In 6/8 time, however, 8th notes are usually not beamed at all.

Example 3.12. Beaming in 3/4 time

16th notes are always beamed according to the beat they are in. The beams never extend between beats (Example 3.13.) This is true in all time signatures.

Example 3.13. 16th Notes in 4/4 Time

In 6/8 time, each 8th note technically gets one beat (even though we tend to subdivide it in two.) Therefore, 16th notes are beamed accordingly (Example 3.14.)

Example 3.14. Beaming of 16th Notes in 6/8 time

When 8th and 16th notes are used together, the beaming should be done by the beat as well (Example 3.15.) This is also applicable to all time signatures.

Example 3.15. Beaming of Eighth and 16th Notes Together

32nd notes and smaller are still beamed by the beat (Example 3.16.) Even when they are mixed with 8th and 16th notes, the notes will be beamed together by the beat (Example 3.17.) This is also true for all time signatures.

Example 3.16. Beaming of 32nd Notes

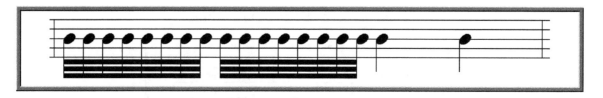

Example 3.17. Beaming of 32nd, 16th, and 8th Notes

Understanding Rhythmic Subdivision

One of the most difficult concepts for non-drummers to grasp is that of rhythmic subdivision. Composers and arrangers often struggle when attempting to notate a highly syncopated rhythm, for instance.

A simple tool that will help any musician or composer immensely is the metronome. Every musician, regardless of his or her instrument, should own a metronome. Many of the better devices available will also play 8th and 16th note subdivisions. This can be extremely helpful when attempting to notate a syncopated rhythm.

A suggested technique for figuring out a syncopated rhythm is to slow the metronome down, enable the 8th or 16th note subdivisions, sing or tap the rhythm you wish to notate, then write it down. Remember that each beat (in 4/4) is divided into two 8th notes, four 16th notes, eight 32nd notes, and so on.

First, create a grid similar to the one in Figure 3.4 below.

Beats:	1				2				3				4			
Subdivisions:																

Figure 3.4. Rhythmic Subdivision Grid

If your rhythm is longer than one measure, lengthen the grid accordingly. If the rhythmic passage is rather long, you may want to work on a few measures at a time.

With your metronome on at a very slow tempo, sing or tap the rhythm, writing a dot in the appropriate column for the beginning of each note. You may want to start by only notating the notes that start on a beat, then move on to 8th note subdivisions, followed by 16th note subdivisions, and so on. Once you are finished with this, you may wish to go back and fill in the columns after the beginning of each note, so you can figure out how long each one is.

A page full of one-measure grids is provided at the end of this chapter. Feel free to make copies of the page, so you can use them in the future.

> **Written Assignment 3.2:** Identify the rhythmic errors in the workbook example. Notate the correct rhythms in the blank measure to the right of each:

Lead Sheets

Writing a lead sheet arrangement of a song may seem at first glance a rather simple process, but it is not always as simple as it seems. True, it is easier to write out one lead sheet than write a separate part for each instrument, but some sacrifices may be required in exchange for this convenience. One standard type of lead sheet is the type that contains the melody, lyrics and chord changes, all on one staff, as illustrated in Example 3.18.

Example 3.18. Single-Staff Lead Sheet with Melody.

This type of lead sheet is generally thought to be the easiest to read, because everything is in close proximity. Of course, some may ask: "Why does the band need the lyrics written out? Why not just give them the chord changes?" Many instrumentalists prefer having the lyrics in front of them as a visual cue, just in case they get lost. However, if your band would rather not have to see the lyrics, there is another technique that will be revealed shortly.

The single-staff lead sheet is not as useful, however, if the band needs to play complex rhythmic figures which differ from the melody. In such a case, 2 staves may be required, with the upper staff devoted to melody and lyrics, and the lower to chord changes and rhythms. There are standard techniques for rhythmic notation of chord symbols. When the band is expected to play "time," i.e., the standard beat, with chord changes generally on the beat, a series of diagonal forward-slashes are utilized, one for each beat (Example 3.19.)

Example 3.19. Rhythmic Notation for Playing "Time"

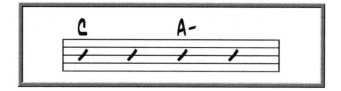

The above would indicate to the band that a C major chord is to be played on beats one and two, and an A minor chord on beats three and four. For more complex rhythmic notation, a mix of the forward-slash technique and standard notation is used (the unwieldy term "forward-slash" will continue to be used in this chapter, so as not to confuse the reader with the subject of the following chapter, "slash chords.") In this method, a forward-slash is used as the note head for any note value of a quarter note or smaller, and a stem is attached, along with a flag, if necessary. For whole- and half-note rhythms, a diamond is used as the note head (Example 3.20.)

35

Example 3.20. Techniques for Slash Rhythmic Notation

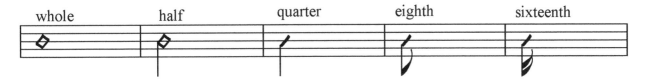

Both techniques may be used interchangeably, and it is acceptable for a measure to include forward-slashes with and without stems. However, standard rules for rhythmic notation must be followed. Example 3.21 illustrates a typical four-measure phrase utilizing this technique.

Example 3.21. Two-Stave Lead Sheet With Melody.

In the first measure of example 3.21, the first two beats are notated with forward-slashes. As the next chord change does not occur until the "and" of beat three, the first eighth-note of beat three must be accounted for by an eighth-note forward-slash. A forward-slash without a stem is always used to indicate the note value on which the time signature is based, which in this case is the quarter note. Consequently, it would not be acceptable to use a forward-slash without a stem on beat three.

In situations where there is no need to notate the melody, a lead sheet may consist solely of chord changes and rhythmic notation, as illustrated in Example 3.22.

Example 3.22. Single-Line Lead Sheet with No Melody.

Anatomy of a Lead Sheet

Example 3.23 illustrates the first page of a typical single-staff lead sheet with melody. Important items are labeled by text preceded by an asterisk (*).

Example 3.23. Sample Lead Sheet

The first page should contain the title and composer/lyricist name on top. The first line of music on this page is approximately two inches from the top of the page. In handwritten lead sheets on commercial staff paper, it is common to skip the first one or 2 staves. The top staff on the following pages should be about one inch from the top of the

37

page. The style and/or tempo should be indicated above the time and key signature on the first staff. As is typical, the time signature only needs to be indicated in the first measure, unless there are meter changes within the song. In addition, the clef and key signature only need to appear on the top of each page, unless there are key or clef changes.

Measure numbers and/or letters should be used to label sections. If measure numbers are used, it is best to label the first measure of each system, and a measure number with a circle or square around it should label the beginning of each section. If letters are the preferred method, it is also advisable to label the beginning of each system with a letter and measure number. For instance, if the 5th measure of section "A" is at the beginning of a new system, it would be numbered "A5," but would not be enclosed by a circle or square. Furthermore, a double bar should be used at the end of each section, including the introduction. For ease of navigation, it is best to plan your lead sheet so that each section begins on the left side of the page, at the beginning of a new system.

If you are creating your lead sheets by hand, rather than computer, it is imperative that a straightedge is used for measure lines and note stems. A messy lead sheet is usually difficult to read. It is also a good idea to draw the measure lines in advance, using a ruler to ensure that they are evenly spaced. The last measure line on each system should be at the very end of the staff. Extra staff space at the end of a system can often be confusing. Some professional copyists who hand-write charts prefer to stagger the placement of measure lines from system to system (except the lines at the beginning and end of the system.) They feel that if the measures line up exactly it is more difficult to read. This, however, is up to the individual.

Chord symbol placement is very important in a lead sheet. The chords must be placed above the correct rhythm on the staff. If there is only one chord in a measure, and it begins on beat one, the chord symbol must be placed at the beginning of the measure, above beat one. If one chord is to be played for several measures, it only needs to be indicated the first time it is played. In example 3.19, one-measure repeats are indicated in measures two and three. However, these measures could also contain forward-slashes, and it would still be clear that the "E" chord should be played in measures two and three (example 3.24.)

Example 3.24. Chord Symbol – Four Measures

However, if the chord continues on a new system, it is a good idea to reiterate the chord symbol at the beginning of the new system, as in example 3.25.

Example 3.25. Chord Symbol – Two Staff Systems

How a Lead Sheet Becomes a Lead Sheet Arrangement

Lead sheets are in essence a bare-bones presentation of the melody, chords and lyrics. One may not necessarily call them arrangements. However, a lead sheet can include an introduction and an ending, as well as some specific instructions for the band, and may even be written in a custom key suited for a particular singer. In such a case, a lead sheet could be called an arrangement.

When writing a lead sheet for a song someone else has written, the most common sources are fake books, sheet music, and transcription. Sheet music often follows the arrangement of the song as it was originally recorded, and this is often preferred. Of course, if you transcribe the song from the original recording, you can also arrange it as it was originally recorded. Fake books, on the other hand, contain lead sheets for songs, and rarely include an introduction or ending.

Introductions and Endings

If you have heard a recording of the song and wish to model the lead sheet after it, your best solution is to transcribe the intro and ending. However, if that is impossible, there are other options available. An introduction should usually be four to eight measures long. Often, the beginning of the song or the end of a particular section can provide the material for an introduction. For instance, *Please Please Me* by the Beatles begins with the last four measures of the bridge. The introduction of *Without You* by Harry Nilsson consists of the first measure of the song repeated twice.

Other standard intro chord progressions are the 1-6m-2m-5, 1-6m-4-5, 1-4-1-5, or any combination thereof. Of course, *I Saw Her Standing There* begins with a 1 chord "vamp" for four measures. A blues song may begin with one "chorus," or the entire 12-measure form played one time through.

Endings are only difficult if the song in question "fades out" on the original recording. This indicates that even the composer couldn't think of a decent ending. The first step is to listen to a live recording, if possible. If not, one safe bet is to end on the 1 chord, either held (example 3.7) or abrupt (example 3.8.)

Notation for Low Voices

If the melody is to be sung by a male or a low alto, it can be written transposed up an octave on the treble clef, to avoid excessive ledger lines below the staff. In many choral arrangements, the tenor part is notated this way, and a treble clef with an "8" on the bottom is used (Figure 3.4.)

Figure 3.5. Clef Used for Tenor Voice

Chord Charts

There are many advantages to including the melody and lyrics in a lead sheet. For instance, if the band or accompanist gets lost, they can find their place in the music by listening to the singer and looking for that lyric on the lead sheet. However, there may be times when it is not practical or necessary to write out the melody and lyrics. In those situations, a chord chart is sufficient. There are several ways to write chord charts. If the chord progression does not include any syncopated rhythms, the chart does not even need to be written on staff paper. It can be written or typed on blank paper in one of the following ways (Examples 3.26-3.27):

Example 3.26. Chord Chart with Forward-Slashes

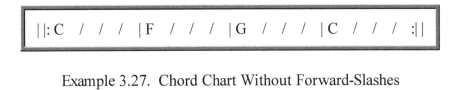

Example 3.27. Chord Chart Without Forward-Slashes

Note that even repeat signs can be indicated with the use of the colon (:) if the chord chart is produced using a computer word-processing program. It may be necessary to hand-write some musical symbols on the printed version, however. If the computer being used has a music notation program, such as Finale, those fonts may be available in the word-processing program as well. In addition, the Microsoft Bookshelf fonts include many musical symbols.

When using the chord chart format illustrated in example 3.27, it is a good idea to use measure repeat symbols if a chord is repeated for more than one measure (Example 3.28.)

Example 3.28. Measure Repeat Symbol

If forward-slashes are used, however, the measure repeat symbol is unnecessary, as in Example 3.29:

Example 3.29. Forward-Slashes and Repeated Chords

Forward-Slashes in Chord Charts

Forward-slashes are not always necessary in chord charts. For instance, if the chord progression consists of only one chord per measure, or two chords per measure with the chords falling on beats one and three, no slashes are necessary.

Example 3.30. No Forward-Slashes Required

However, if any chords fall on beats two and four, slashes should be used.

Example 3.31. Forward-Slashes Required

If the chord progression includes syncopated rhythms, it may be necessary to present the chord chart on staff paper, placing the chord symbol above the staff, and using a mixture of forward-slashes and slash rhythmic notation in the staff. A chord chart with syncopated rhythms can be notated by hand on a blank sheet of paper, as illustrated in Example 3.32.

41

Example 3.32. Chord Chart Without Staff

Creating an Overview or Outline

     Before you begin your lead sheet, it is a good idea to sketch out an outline for the song. Make decisions regarding the length of intros, transitions, and endings, and figure out where repeats, to coda, and codas should happen. Then, lay out the lead sheet, putting in measure lines, section letters, etc. It is best that this be done before any notes are printed on the paper (or computer screen.) It is important to be mindful of the rhythmic and harmonic complexity of the song. If the melody contains many 8th- and 16th-note rhythms, 4 measures per system may be too much. Similarly, if there are four or more chords per measure, 3 measures per system may work better.

     This technique is also useful during the composition process. An outline of the song form before you even begin composing will help tremendously. It may not be necessary to lay out the lead sheet early in the process, but a brief sketch of the form of the song may be helpful.

Lead Sheet/Chord Chart Checklist

   ✓ Make sure forward-slashes are diagonal, and evenly spaced within the measure. Use a straightedge.

   ✓ Bar lines at the beginning and end of each system

   ✓ Plan measures ahead of time, and don't leave any space at the end of a system (unless you have staff paper where the staves cover the entire page)

   ✓ Keep your lyrics and chords as straight as possible; use a ruler underneath your lyrics to keep them straight

   ✓ Make sure to use staff paper with the staves far enough apart to accommodate lyrics and chord changes. Use 10- or 8-stave paper rather than 12-stave

   ✓ If using section letters, section "A" should begin where the melody begins, after the introduction.

   ✓ Don't forget the use of "simile"

   ✓ Each page should be on a separate sheet; the whole idea is to reduce page turns. If you have multiple pages, you can tape them together.

   ✓ Make sure D.S. and Coda signs are easy to spot

Written Assignment 3.3: Identify all of the mistakes in the lead sheet example.
Written Assignment 3.4: Write a lead sheet from a standard pop sheet music arrangement.
   Include an introduction and ending, if it is not already included.

42

Nashville Number Charts In Depth

Nashville number charts share some similarities to lead sheets, but there are also many differences in terms of format. Example 3.33 illustrates a typical Nashville chart.

Example 3.33. Sample Nashville Number Chart

Intro:

‖   1   4 | 5   6m | 1   4 | 5˙   ‖

Verse:

‖:   1   b7 | 4   b6 | 1   6m | 2m   5 |

①——

| 1   b7 | 4   b6 | 5   6 | 2   5   :‖

②——

| 1   b7 | 4   4m | 1   5 | 1˙   ‖

Bridge:

‖   3 | 6m } {> 6 | 2   b3 | b5   7 |

| 3 | 6m } {> 6 | 2   5 1 | 5   ⟨5⁺⟩⌢ ‖
                                              / / / /

Chorus:

‖   1   b7 | 4   b6 | 5   6m | 2m   5 |

| 1   1/b7 | 4/6   ⟨5sus⟩⌢⟨5sus⟩   5   ⟨1⟩   ‖

On the following page is an explanation of the different symbols and formatting used in Example 3.33:

Symbols and Formatting Used in Nashville Charts

e   Sections of the song are labeled, rather than measure numbers.

e   The dot on the top of the 5 chord in the 4th measure of the intro indicates that the chord is played on beat one, followed by three beats of rest.

e   The verse has a repeat sign; the first ending begins at measure 5, and the second ending at measure 9. Ending numbers are circled, and a straight line extends to the last measure of the ending.

e   There is also a dot over the 1 chord at the end of the second ending. Once again, the chord is played once, followed by three beats of rest.

e   In measures 2 and 6 of the bridge, there is a 6m chord followed by two quarter rests and a > sign in front of the 6 chord. The > sign indicates an 8th-note anticipation. In other words, rather than the two beats of rest indicated, there is only one and one-half, and the chord is played on the "and" of three.

e   Measure 7 of the bridge contains four slashes beneath the chords, indicating the beats on which those chords should be played.

e   In measure 8 of the bridge, the 5+ chord has a diamond around it. That means that the chord should be held. If there were not fermata over the chord, the chord would be held as a half note on beats 3 and 4.

e   In measures 6 and 7 of the chorus, the 5sus chord should be treated as two half notes tied together.

e   In the final measure of the chorus, the 1 chord is a held whole note.

One other note of interest regarding Nashville charts: they do not use the standard coda. Instead, the coda is usually labeled as the "Ending." The phrase "*Last X to ending" is placed above or below the first measure of the section which will not be played the last time through. Perhaps it should be explained another way: In a normal lead sheet, the "to coda" sign is placed at the end of the measure in which the musicians will jump to the coda. In a Nashville chart, however, the indication is placed at the beginning of the measure *after* the bar in which the band jumps to the coda. Are you confused yet?

Unfortunately, there is no set standard for Nashville charts, and there are probably many additional formats used in Nashville. Just remember, any chart should be easy to follow. One additional option: programs like Finale allow the user to substitute Nashville numbers for chord symbols, enabling composers to use conventional lead sheet format with Nashville numbers. It is best to find the method that best suits your situation.

Written Assignment 3.5: Write a Nashville number chart for a pop song.

Rhythmic Subdivision Grid

Beats:	1				2				3				4			
Subdivisions:																

Beats:	1				2				3				4			
Subdivisions:																

Beats:	1				2				3				4			
Subdivisions:																

Beats:	1				2				3				4			
Subdivisions:																

Beats:	1				2				3				4			
Subdivisions:																

Beats:	1				2				3				4			
Subdivisions:																

Beats:	1				2				3				4			
Subdivisions:																

Beats:	1				2				3				4			
Subdivisions:																

Beats:	1				2				3				4			
Subdivisions:																

Beats:	1				2				3				4			
Subdivisions:																

Beats:	1				2				3				4			
Subdivisions:																

Beats:	1				2				3				4			
Subdivisions:																

Checklist of Assignments for Chapter 3

✓ **Written Assignment 3.1:** Analyze the form of two pop songs from different genres or eras.

✓ **Written Assignment 3.2:** Identify the rhythmic errors in the examples and notate the correct rhythms in the measure on the right.

✓ **Written Assignment 3.3:** Identify all of the mistakes in the lead sheet example.

✓ **Written Assignment 3.4:** Write a lead sheet from a standard pop sheet music arrangement. Include an introduction and ending, if it is not already included.

✓ **Written Assignment 3.5:** Write a Nashville number chart for a pop song.

47

4

COMPOSING MELODIES

The craft of writing a melody is often overlooked in some of today's popular music styles. Modern pop songwriters will often compose a chord progression or bass line before they even begin thinking of a melody. In the early 20th Century, however, melody was the most important aspect of popular song. As mentioned in an earlier chapter, some early pop composers didn't even know how to compose a chord progression. They did know how to craft a melody, however. Even in today's world, the ability to write a good melody is an important skill for any composer.

The Elements of Melody

All melodies, good and bad, have a few common elements. The smallest element of a melody is an individual note. A motive is a series of two or more notes, and a phrase is a series of two or more motives. A phrase usually continues until one of the motives creates a strong cadence, giving a logical ending to the phrase. The following phrase may be a repeat of that phrase, or a brand new one. A phrase may make up an entire verse, another phrase the chorus, and another phrase the bridge. However, each section of a song can also consist of two or more phrases.

Composing a Motive

An excellent method for writing a melody is to start by composing a motive. A motive can be any combination of two or more notes, and is usually 1 or 2 measures long. It is important to carefully consider the intervals to be used in the motive. Should you use stepwise intervals or leaps, or a combination of the two? A motive composed entirely of leaps may be difficult to sing, depending on the size of the leaps. Generally, melodies containing leaps usually contain some stepwise intervals as well.

Often, a leap will be followed by stepwise motion in the opposite direction. This lends a sense of balance to a motive.

48

Some intervals seem to evoke an emotional reaction in the listener. The minor 6th, for example, is often used in sad ballads. Minor and major 7ths can be very intense, also carrying a hint of dark romanticism. Tritones are often thought of as gothic, frightening intervals. However, the melody of the love song *Maria*, from West Side Story by Leonard Bernstein, begins with a tritone. Take the time to play through each of the intervals slowly, and see if they elicit an emotional response in you.

It is also important to consider whether the motive will be chromatic, based on one or more scales/modes, or a combination of the two. If we are to believe the ancient Greeks, certain modes evoke an emotional response from the listener. In playing through the modes and scales, you may find one that fits your needs. Be aware that a completely chromatic motive may be more difficult to harmonize. Chromaticism in a melody can be very powerful, however, creating tension and emotional intensity.

The contour of the motive is also an important element to ponder. The term contour when applied to a motive (or a phrase or entire melody) is used to describe the amount and order of ascending and descending intervals, as well as the size of those intervals. Will the motive consist of ascending intervals, descending intervals, or a combination of the two? We often tend to equate ascending lines with increasing intensity, and descending lines with decreasing intensity. When ascending leaps are used, the intensity increases more profoundly. Of course, the range of the singing voice, and the area of the vocal range the melody is in, or *tessitura*, plays an important part as well.

The technique of following a leap by stepwise motion in the opposite direction will aid in creating effective melodic contour. For instance, an upward leap followed by downward stepwise motion will cause increased intensity followed by relaxation. Of course, stepwise motion followed by a leap in the opposite direction is also an option.

Building a Phrase

After the motives have been composed, then comes the task of beginning to build a phrase. Once the first motive is stated, you have several options: 1.) You can compose a second motive to follow the first one, or 2.) You can develop the first motive using the techniques described in Table 10.1 below. Even if you choose to compose a new motive, you may wish to repeat one or both of the motives again, and the techniques in Table 4.1 can be used as well.

Table 4.1. Techniques for Melodic Development

Technique	Description
Sequence	A common compositional technique, in which the melodic motive is repeated at a different pitch level. The intervals can either be exactly the same in relation to the new pitch (we will call this an exact sequence,) or they can be changed to fit the underlying harmony or scale/mode (diatonic sequence.) This is one of the most effective melodic devices available, and it is widely used.
Repetition	An exact repetition of the melodic motive can also be extremely effective.
Rhythmic Repetition	A repetition of the same rhythm, but with different, often unrelated, pitches. The motive may end on the ending pitch of the original motive, or a different pitch.
Elongation or Diminution	Repeating the motive with either longer or shorter note values works well.
Inversion, Retrograde, and Retrograde Inversion	Inverting or reversing the motive is also useful. An inversion is achieved by using the same or similar intervals moving in the opposite direction. When inverting a motive, it may be an exact inversion (the same intervals moving in the opposite direction) or a diatonic inversion (conforming to the scale/mode.) Retrograde motion is achieved by reversing the motive, starting with the last pitch and going backwards. Reversing the motive and then inverting it achieve a Retrograde Inversion. This can also be an exact or diatonic retrograde inversion.
Melodic Variation	Changing some of the notes when repeating the motive is yet another effective technique, especially replacing a scalewise interval with a leap.
Rhythmic Variation	One can vary the rhythmic presentation of the motive, and the rhythmic placement of the motive in relation to the beat.
Combining Two or More Motives	It is very effective to state several melodic motives at first, switching between the two or combining the two in various ways.
Thematic Development	Along the lines of melodic variation. After stating the motive, each repetition may include a few more notes, so that it gradually "morphs" into a more complex theme. A series of notes can lead up to the motive as well, or a series of notes can follow the motive to lead to the next motive.

The following examples illustrate the above techniques using a 1-measure motive:

Example 4.1 A 1-measure motive

Example 4.2 Sequence (up a major 2nd)

Example 4.3 Repetition

Example 4.4 Rhythmic Repetition

Example 4.5 Elongation and Diminution

Example 4.6 Retrograde and Inversion

*(transposed up an octave to reduce ledger lines)

51

Example 4.7 Retrograde Inversion

Diatonic: Exact:

Example 4.8 Melodic Variation

Example 4.9 Rhythmic Variation

Example 4.10 Combining Two or More Motives

1st motive: 2nd motive: Repeat of 1st motive: Rhythmic repetition of 1st motive:

Example 4.11 Thematic Development

A series of notes leading to the restatement of motive:

Of course, all of the techniques mentioned above are interchangeable and combined in different ways. For instance, an inversion, retrograde, or retrograde inversion can also begin on a different pitch than the original, creating a sort of sequence. Melodic variation can also include rhythmic variation, or two combined motives combined to create a sequence. The possibilities are endless.

Example 4.12 illustrates a diatonic and exact retrograde inversion beginning on the same pitch as the original motive:

Example 4.12 Retrograde Inversion Beginning on the Same Pitch

Diatonic: Exact:

How does one know when a phrase is complete, you may ask. This is up to the whim of the individual composer. Cadence is just as important in a melody as it is in a chord progression. If the melody seems to suggest some sort of authentic cadence, where it would be logical to move on to another phrase or repeat the entire phrase again, it probably constitutes a complete phrase. A motive that ends on the root or third of the 1 chord will generally sound like an authentic cadence, depending on the notes which precede it. Of course, ending on the fifth of the 1 chord can suggest an authentic cadence, but it can also suggest a half cadence as well. Consequently, you have to keep this in mind when composing the phrase.

Generally, the final note of each motive should "want" to keep going somewhere else, if you are not ready to finish the phrase. If the final note of the motive is not a chord tone of the 1 chord or the 5 chord, it is probably not the best place to end the phrase. If the end of the phrase suggests a half cadence, the composer has an opportunity to repeat the phrase again, ending on the root or third of the 1 chord the second time to lend a stronger cadential ending to the phrase. However, in a verse consisting of two phrases, it is quite common to end both phrases with a half cadence. This will provide stronger forward motion into the chorus. If there is a modulation to a new key within a phrase or between two phrases, the point before the modulation should contain notes that will lead into the new key. A chord tone belonging to the 5 chord in the new key is the typical method.

You must also think of the contour of the phrase itself. This is, of course determined by the range, and to a lesser extent, the rhythmic complexity of the melody. Does the melodic contour move up, then down, then up again, or up, then down again, or only up? Any of those options are viable. A motive consisting mostly of descending intervals can follow a motive consisting mostly of ascending intervals. Similarly, a motive consisting of ascending stepwise intervals can be followed by a motive consisting of descending stepwise intervals, followed by an ascending motive consisting of stepwise intervals and leaps, and so on. Thus, the contour of the phrase can move up, then down, then up a little more, then down, etc. This can also set up a sort of "question and answer" relationship between motives, where the ascending motive is the question and the descending motive is the answer.

Rhythm is also another important element in melody. If there is a change in rhythmic complexity, it should move from simple to more complex. Rhythmic placement of notes is also crucial. An authentic cadence will generally end on a strong beat, such as one or three. Beat one is, of course, the strongest beat in any measure. Motives ending on weak beats or subdivisions of beats will generally "want" to move on to another motive before the phrase is complete. A motive ending on a long note, even if the note begins on a weak beat, may indicate the ending of a phrase as well, depending on the note.

Rhythmic placement of the beginning of a phrase is also very important. A useful method for beginning a phrase is using a motive that begins on a *Pickup Note*, usually near beat four of the measure. A pickup note is a strong indication of the beginning of a phrase. Typically, the pickup note will not be the tonic of the key, especially if there is a 1 chord on beat one of the following measure. Pickup notes are often a step above or below the note on beat one of the next measure, but it can be almost any note. Pickup notes may even begin on the "and" of beats three or four. There can also be more than one pickup note.

Texture is also important to the building of a phrase. Early motives in the phrase can consist of fewer notes and more rests, and later motives more notes. Remember that rests are as important as notes. A phrase with many notes and few rests can quickly grow tedious.

The rhythmic placement of rests is important as well. All of the above factors tend to determine the forward motion and intensity-building aspects of a phrase.

Length of a phrase is very important. Traditionally, phrase lengths tend to be in multiples of four. Four, eight, or sixteen measure phrases are quite common. A 12-bar blues may consist of three four-measure phrases, or one twelve-measure phrase. Odd phrase lengths are not impossible, but be aware that they will affect the form of the song. Phrases usually consist of an even number of motives, but there can be exceptions to this as well.

An 8-measure phrase can consist of four 2-measure motives or two 4-measure motives. Eight 1-measure motives are also possible, but this can overly repetitive. However, another common configuration is an 8-measure phrase consisting of two 2-measure motives followed by one 4-measure motive.

Composers often use motives in which the length of the motive is smaller than one measure, or somewhere between one and two measures in length. The typical technique is to fill in the remainder of the unfinished measure with rests. However, motives of non-standard lengths can be repeated or sequenced until an even number of measures is reached, or repeated/sequenced several times, followed by rests until the end of the measure, if needed. The rhythmic placement of the motive will change with each repetition, crossing the bar line. This can be extremely effective for building intensity.

Examples 4.13 and 4.14 illustrate two phrases of a typical pop ballad. Example 4.13 displays the two primary motives.

Example 4.13 Two Motives Used in Example 4.14

Example 4.14 Two Phrases of a Pop Ballad Melody

Both of the phrases begin with an 8th-note pickup. The first phrase ends in measures 5-8 with a thematic development of motive 2, essentially elongating the motive to 3 measures followed by a measure of rest. This first phrase ends with a half cadence.

In measures 9 and 10, adding several shorter notes varies motive 1. Measures 11-14 begin with what looks like a sequence of motive 2. However, the motive develops a bit by using the beginning rhythm of the motive at the end of the development. The rhythmic displacement of this shortened motive helps to build intensity. A third, simpler motive can end the second phrase, most likely with a half cadence.

Since both phrases end with half cadences, there is continual forward motion. This would probably be the verse of the song, and the chorus would probably end with an authentic cadence.

Melodic Contour of Phrases

The contour of each phrase ought to aid in leading to the next phrase. It is a good idea to produce a visual representation, or graph, of the contour of your melody. In fact, some composers will graph out a proposed melodic contour before they even compose the melody, using the graph as a guide. There are many methods for graphing melodic contour. In the illustration below is one such method.

First, assign numbers to each pitch (Table 4.2.)

Table 4.2 Numbers Assigned to Pitches for Graphic Analysis

1	C (below middle C)	13	Middle C	25	C (above middle C)
2	C♯	14	C♯	26	C♯
3	D	15	D	27	D
4	D♯	16	D♯	28	D♯
5	E	17	E	29	E
6	F	18	F	30	F
7	F♯	19	F♯	31	F♯
8	G	20	G	32	G
9	G♯	21	G♯	33	G♯
10	A	22	A	34	A
11	A♯	23	A♯	35	A♯
12	B	24	B	36	B

Next, using your number scale, graph out the pitches of the melody. It doesn't matter whether you can tell the exact pitches on the graph. The purpose here is to see the overall contour of your melody. We will call our graph a *Graphic Analysis*. Figure 4.1 illustrates a graphic analysis of the melody in Example 4.14.

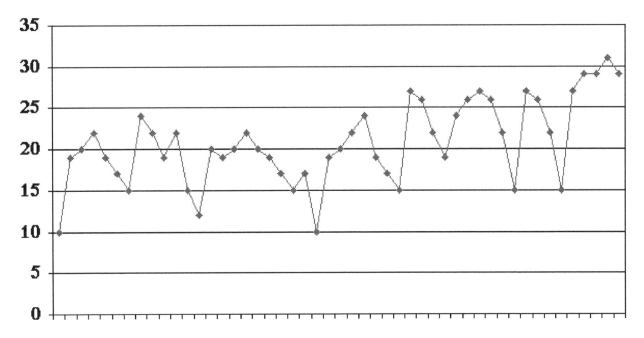

Figure 4.1 Graphic Analysis of the Melody in Example 4.14

The graph reveals that the melody slowly builds to a high point at the end. It is not building constantly, however. There are some dips as well as peaks in the graph. There are other methods of analyzing the contour of a melody. For instance, a staff could act as an analysis tool instead of a graph. Choose the method that is easiest for you.

> **Written Assignment 4.1:** Using the motive pictured, illustrate the melodic development techniques.
>
> **Written Assignment 4.2:** Perform graphic analyses on the melodies of two of your favorite pop songs.

Putting Together the Song

Once the phrases are completed, it is time to think about the form of each section and the song as a whole. One phrase may constitute one verse of the song, or the verse can use more than one phrase. As implied earlier, the length of the phrases may help determine the form of a song. One section of a song will often be 16, 32, or even 64 measures long.

If the melody in the verse and chorus are similar, you may wish to compose a bridge with a completely different melody. This is quite common, as the design of the bridge is to take the listener by surprise, create interest, and build intensity.

It is common, when composing, to write the lyrics and the melody at the same time. Often a melody will suggest a lyric, and vice versa. Of course, having the lyrics in mind may help you decide where to end a phrase as well.

The contour of each phrase in the verses should not exceed the contour of the chorus, for that is where the verses ought to lead. If there is a bridge, it often has a slightly higher level of intensity than the chorus that occurred before it. Once again, it may help to perform a graphic analysis of your melody.

Cadence is also an important consideration, even at this point. The chorus will usually have a stronger ending cadence than the verse. For instance, you may end each verse with a descending authentic or half cadence, and each chorus with an ascending authentic cadence.

> **Listening Assignment 4.1:** Find three examples of pop songs that use the techniques described above in the melodies. List each song, and list the techniques used. Bring a recording of one of them to play in class

Harmonizing a Melody

Harmonizing a melody you have composed can be extremely simple or extremely difficult. If the melody is tonal, it will most likely suggest the harmony. Even chromatic alterations (notes outside the key) may suggest a chord. Once you begin composing a chord progression, be prepared to alter the melody somewhat, as you may find it necessary. In general, the melody note should be either a chord tone or a member of the scale on which one bases the melody. There are other alternatives discussed in a later chapter.

When all else fails, use your ears.

Writing a Melody to a Chord Progression

The real test for a composer is writing an interesting melody to a chord progression. Here, the key word is "interesting". Many pop songwriters compose chord progressions first, adding melodies later. Often, the melodies are not as interesting as the chord progression.

Unfortunately, there is no formula to this, and, once again, you must use your ears. After playing through the progression a few times, you may find that a melody begins to come to mind. However, if that does not work, concentrate on the first one or two measures of the progression, and see if you can come up with a motive. Then try to develop the motive using the rest of the progression as a guide.

> **Written Assignment 4.3:** Compose a melody to one of the 16-measure chord progressions you composed earlier in the course. The melody should demonstrate the techniques learned in this chapter.
>
> **Project 1.0:** Compose a 30-second commercial jingle, writing the melody and lyrics first, and then adding chords. The jingle should include a vocal throughout, with an intro of no more than one measure, and no spoken voice-over. Use an existing product, or make one up. To determine how many measures a 30-second jingle will be, take the tempo and divide it by 2. That will be the number of beats of which your melody should consist.

Checklist of Assignments for Chapter 4

- ✓ **Written Assignment 4.1:** Using the motives pictured, illustrate the melodic development techniques.
- ✓ **Written Assignment 4.2:** Perform graphic analyses on the melodies of two of your favorite pop songs.
- ✓ **Listening Assignment 4.1:** Find three examples of pop songs that use the techniques described above in the melodies. List each song, and list the techniques used. Bring a recording of one of them to play in class
- ✓ **Written Assignment 4.3:** Compose a melody to one of the 16-measure chord progressions you composed earlier in the course. The melody should demonstrate the techniques learned in this chapter.
- ✓ **Project 1.0:** Compose a 30-second commercial jingle, writing the melody and lyrics first, and then adding chords. The jingle should include a vocal throughout, with an intro of no more than one measure, and no spoken voice-over. Use an existing product, or make one up. To determine how many measures a 30-second jingle will be, take the tempo and divide it by 2. That will be the number of beats of which your melody should consist.

5

SLASH CHORDS/UPPER STRUCTURES

A *Slash Chord* is one chord or triad superimposed over another chord, triad, or bass note. Slash chords often occur in pop music, and there is an important rule to follow in assigning a name to such a chord. Label a B♭ triad with a C in the bass as B♭/C; or notate, a B♭ triad over a C triad (known as a *Polychord*, or one chord superimposed over another) like a fraction, with a horizontal line between the two (Figure 5.1.)

Figure 5.1 Slash Chord for a B♭ Triad over a C triad

A slash chord can include any type of chord, not just a triad. The top chord in either form is often referred to as the *Upper Structure*.

The triad-over-bass note form of slash chord is the type most commonly used in pop music. Perhaps the most prevalent use for slash chords is that of forming a chord inversion. For instance, a C/E chord symbol would indicate the chord is in first inversion, or a C/G symbol would indicate a second inversion chord. This type of slash chord is particularly useful when there is a scalewise bass line upon which the song is built.

Most Commonly Used Slash Chords

Practically any chord-over-bass note combination occurs in today's pop music, especially in modal jazz. However, there are some standard slash chords used more frequently than others are. Examples 5.1-5.7 illustrate some of the most common slash chords.

Example 5.1 Major Upper Structures

Example 5.2 Minor Upper Structures

Example 5.3 Diminished Upper Structures

Example 5.4 Augmented Upper Structures

61

Example 5.5 Sus2 Upper Structures

Csus2/E   Csus2/Eb   Csus2/Bb   Csus2/A   Csus2/Ab

Upon closer examination, some of these slash chords could be labeled in other ways. For instance, the Csus2/E is a C chord with the third in the bass and an added D. In reality, it is not a typical "sus2" because it includes the third. However, the composer can insure that the pianist will only play the third in the left hand by calling it a Csus2/E. In fact, a C5/E chord could produce a similar effect, if desired. A composer can use slash chords to indicate a certain voicing, sometimes "spicing up" the sound of an otherwise typical chord.

Note that the sus2 slash chords do not exist as inversions. The only inversion available would be Csus2/G, which is actually a Gsus4 chord. Thus, it is useless and confusing to call it Csus2/G.

Ear-Training Assignment 5.1: Learn to identify the slash chords pictured in Example 5.5.

Using Slash Chords in a Chord Progression

Use slash chords as passing chords. For example, a chord progression with a descending or ascending scalewise bass line will often sound strange if all of the chords are root-position chords. Examples 5.6 illustrates slash chords often used with descending scalewise bass lines:

Example 5.6 Descending Diatonic Bass Line with Upper Structures

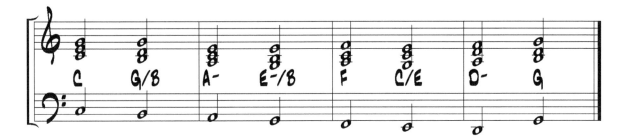

C   G/B   A-   E-/B   F   C/E   D-   G

If the chord progression in Example 5.6 included only root-position diatonic chords, the chord progression would be: 1-7°-6m-5-4-3m-2m-5. The 7°, which normally tends to lead to the 1 chord, would sound especially strange leading to the 6m chord. However, if we disregard the bass notes and analyze the right-hand chord progression, we have 1-5-6m-3m-4-1-2m-5, a chord progression much more pleasing to the ear.

62

Example 5.7 illustrates a similar technique with an ascending scalewise bass line:

Example 5.7 Ascending Diatonic Bass Line with Upper Structures

The chord progression in the right hand is 1-2m-1-4-1-6m-2m-5-1. If the bass line were the root of every chord in a diatonic chord progression, we would have: 1-2m-3m-4-5-6m-6m-7°-1, which would not be as effective. The use of slash chords makes this a much more powerful progression.

Slash Chords and Nashville Numbers

Notating slash chords using Nashville numbering is another option. Since polychords are rarely, if ever, used in the types of music played in Nashville, slash chords are usually notated as fractions, with a horizontal line between the chord number and the root directly underneath. In the Nashville system, use a diagonal slash to indicate beats in a measure where there are more than two chords. Therefore, using a diagonal slash for a slash chord could be confusing. However, this fractional system is almost impossible to achieve with a word processor. A student using a word processor to write Nashville charts can just use the diagonal slashes, leaving more room between chords and diagonal slashes when using them to indicate beats in a measure.

When indicating slash chords in Nashville notation, the number indicating the bass note corresponds to the key, regardless of whether or not the note is in the chord. Example 5.8 illustrates the chord progression in Example 5.6 using Nashville numbers.

Example 5.8 Slash Chord Progression notated with Nashville Numbers

$$| \quad 1 \quad \frac{5}{7} \quad | \quad 6m \quad \frac{3m}{5} \quad | \quad 4 \quad \frac{1}{3} \quad | \quad 2m \quad 5 \quad |$$

Slash Chords and Bass Lines Containing Non-Diatonic Notes

Slash chords are even more effective with bass lines containing notes which are not diatonic to the key, especially if there is some chromatic movement involved (Examples 5.9 and 5.10, including Nashville numbers.)

Example 5.9 Descending Chromatic Bass Lines with Upper Structures

Example 5.10 Ascending Chromatic Bass Line with Upper Structures

The 1-♭7-6-♭6 bass line is quite common in pop music, and Example 5.9 illustrates three different variations. Note that in the second 2-measure example, the C chord remains in the right hand. Even though it may seem that it would sound strange, many composers use this progression quite frequently.

In the preceding examples, slash chords harmonically support a specific bass line. Although we used bass lines which move mostly by whole-steps and half-steps to illustrate this, slash chords can harmonize a moving bass line. It is not uncommon for a composer to come up with a bass line for a song first, and slash chords are often the best way to provide harmony.

A composer may wish to use slash chords in a chord progression played over a static bass note, or a *pedal*. The use of progressions made up of slash chords over a pedal gives one compositional variety. They often lend a certain dramatic effect, building musical intensity with the harmonic tension sometimes created. This can be used quite effectively for an intro, transitions and coda, as found in *8 Days A Week* by the Beatles. However, they can also form the basis for one or more major sections of a song, such as *Turn It On Again* by Genesis or *Takin' It To The Streets* by the Doobie Brothers. In Example 5.11, a series of major triads over a pedal of C lead from an E♭/C to a C major chord in measure 4.

Example 5.11 Upper Structures Over a Pedal

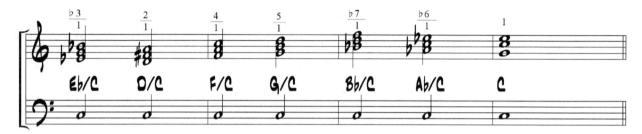

Applying a purely mathematical technique with slash chords, can, at times create surprisingly pleasant results. Devise a bass line made up of two or more alternating intervals or a scale. Then, create a chord progression, using all major or minor triads. This chord progression should begin with the same root as the first bass note, but with roots alternating by two or three different intervals or a different scale. Keep this root movement going until one or both end up back at the original chord. If they end up at the first chord at different times, modify the progression to line them up. This technique can have mixed results, but often the composer will find something they can really use. Example 5.12 illustrates a progression constructed in this manner.

Example 5.12 Upper Structure Progression with Alternating Intervals

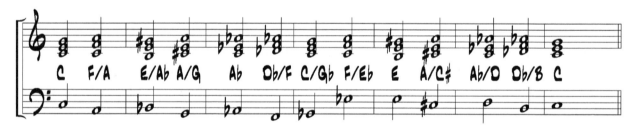

Alternating intervals make up the progression in Example 5.12. The roots of the chords in the right hand move up a perfect 4th, then down a minor 2nd. The bass line moves down a minor 3rd, then up a minor 2nd. The chord progression moves through the pattern twice before lining up with the C in the bass at the end. Note also that some of the chords end up in root position. Some of the combinations are rather dissonant, however, and this progression might not be very useful, except in an avant-garde composition.

Example 5.13 illustrates how some of these ideas could create a more useable pop chord progression.

Example 5.13 Slash Chord Progression

Note that the roots of the right-hand chords move up by intervals of a Perfect 4th through measure 4. In fact, by measure 4, we seem to be in a completely unrelated key. In measure 5, however, everything moves up a half step, ending up on the 5 chord, which eventually leads us back to 1. This progression is more typical of the type used in the bridges of some pop songs, where the seeming modulation through several different keys helps build the intensity of the composition.

Keyboard Assignment 5.1: Play slowly through the slash chord progressions in examples 5.8-5.15, paying close attention to the chord relationships.
Written Assignment 5.1: Analyze the chord progression in the workbook using Nashville numbers. Assume that it begins in the key of C.

Examples of Upper Structures Over a Pedal:

- *8 Days a Week* by the Beatles
- *Turn It On Again* and *Abacab* by Genesis
- *Tom Sawyer* by Rush
- *How Long Has This Been Going On* by Ace
- *Takin' It To The Streets* by the Doobie Brothers
- *Keep On Loving You* by REO Speedwagon

e *Let It Be, Hello Goodbye, Dear Prudence, I Am The Walrus*, and many others by the Beatles
e *White Room* by Cream
e *25 or 6 to 4* by Chicago
e *Minute By Minute* by the Doobie Brothers
e *Anytime* by Brian McKnight
e *Tell Me Something Good* by Chaka Khan and Rufus
e *Something About You* by Level 42
e *Tempted* by Squeeze
e *Sour Girl* by Stone Temple Pilots

Written Assignment 5.2: List five additional examples of pop songs that utilize slash chords (besides the ones in Chapter 4.) Cite the chord progression in each example.

Written Assignment 5.3: Write a 16-measure chord progression that includes five or more slash chords. The progression should consist of at least one chord per measure, and each chord should be different from the one in the measure before or after it. Use chord symbols.

Slash Chords in Performance

The accompanying instrument or musical style of the song usually dictates the use of slash chords. Slash chords are simple to play on piano, but many of them are difficult to play on the guitar. In addition, some slash chords do not sound very pleasant when played by a distorted guitar. Most metal and hard rock guitarists prefer to play chords containing a perfect 5th or perfect 4th between the two lowest notes. Tritone and minor 6th relationships between the two lowest notes are not uncommon in these styles, but their use only as passing chords is more the norm.

In the context of a band, however, it is typical for the bass player to play the bass note in a slash chord, while the guitarist (and sometimes the keyboardist) plays the top chord in root position. A similar technique in bands with two guitarists is one in which one of guitarist doubles the bass line, playing no chords, while the other guitarist plays all of the chords in root position. Both of these methods have different characteristic sounds, and composers should familiarize themselves with these sounds.

Bass players will generally only concern themselves with the bass note on the right side of the slash chord. However, it is important for bass players to understand the chords as well, as there may be times when it is appropriate to begin with the bass note followed by a run consisting of the other notes of the chord.

Slash Chords for Guitar

Any composer who intends a guitarist to play slash chords including the bass note should be aware of the slash chords which are more accessible on the guitar. Examples 5.14 and 5.15 illustrate some of the more commonly used slash chords for the guitarist to play in the first four frets. These examples include the voicing on a grand staff, as well as chord charts with suggested fingerings.

Example 5.14 Common Major Slash Chords for Guitar

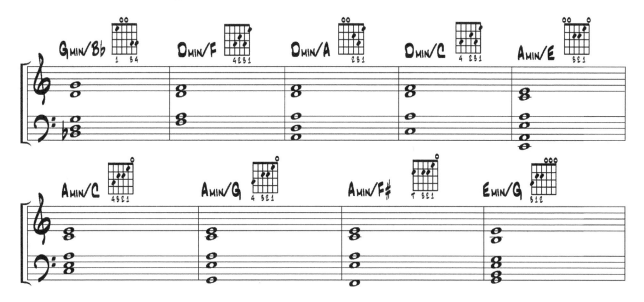

Example 5.15 Common Minor Slash Chords for Guitar

Although the prospects for slash chords on the guitar are somewhat limited, composers writing in non-guitar keys can always ask that the guitarist use a capo. A capo is a bar that when placed above all six strings on any fret, essentially transposes the guitar to another key. When writing for a guitarist using a capo, it is easiest to designate the capoed fret then write the chord symbols as if there were no capo. For example, take a chord progression such as this: Bmin-Bmin/A-E/G♯-A. While this progression is not impossible to play, a simpler, and ultimately more pleasant-sounding, method would be to tell the guitarist to put the capo on the second fret, and notate the progression as: Amin-Amin/G-D/F♯-G. Of course, this is another situation where Nashville numbers would come in handy. Of course, it is always a good idea to make sure that the musicians are familiar with the Nashville system before you use it. The use of capos is more frequent on the acoustic guitar rather than the electric. Some electric guitarists do not even own a capo.

Hard rock styles often use a power chord consisting of a *barre chord* in second inversion. A barre chord is a chord in which the guitarist presses the first finger of the left hand across all of the strings on one of the frets, creating a sort of "human capo". Then he or she uses the remaining fingers to form a chord on the right side of the index finger. Example 5.16 illustrates a barre chord used for a C/G chord.

Example 5.16 Power Chord in second Inversion

Often a guitarist will use this same voicing and play the chord only from the root, leaving out the fifth, which is on the sixth string. However, playing the full second inversion chord through a distortion effect gives even more strength to the power chord, especially if the bass is playing the root below it.

Melodies and Slash Chords

Slash chords can be useful when a composer is attempting to harmonize a melody. If the melody tends to cadence in predictable ways, use slash chords instead. For instance, a 1-4-1-5 progression can become 1-4/6-1/5-5, lending more interest to an otherwise bland progression. Additionally, slash chords may fit the melody where other root-position chords cannot.

Instrumental compositions use slash chord progressions effectively with the top note of the chord voicing serving as the melody. This is especially useful for piano compositions. Instrumental transitions can use the same technique in a song.

Written Assignment 5.4: Compose a solo piano piece of at least 16 measures using mostly slash chords. Notate the chords fully and use chord symbols as well. The top note of each chord should be the melody. Use melodic construction techniques as discussed in the chapter on melody.

Checklist of Assignments for Chapter 5

✓ **Ear-Training Assignment 5.1:** Learn to identify the slash chords pictured.

✓ **Keyboard Assignment 5.1:** Play slowly through the slash chord progressions in examples 5.8-5.15, paying close attention to the chord relationships.

✓ **Written Assignment 5.1:** Analyze the chord progression using Nashville numbers. Assume that it begins in the key of C.

✓ **Written Assignment 5.2:** List five additional examples of pop songs that utilize slash chords (besides the ones listed in Chapter 4.) Cite the chord progression in each example. Use the back of the sheet if necessary.

✓ **Written Assignment 5.3:** Write a 16-measure chord progression that includes five or more slash chords. The progression should consist of at least one chord per measure, and each chord should be different from the one in the measure before or after it. Use chord symbols.

✓ **Written Assignment 5.4:** Compose a solo piano piece of at least 16 measures using mostly slash chords. Notate the chords fully and use chord symbols as well. The top note of each chord should be the melody. Use melodic construction techniques as discussed in the chapter on melody.

6

6TH AND 7TH CHORDS

Pop music often uses 6th and 7th chords, and in jazz, they are generally preferred over simple triads.

7th Chords

A 7th chord is a triad with an added note, a third above the 5th of the chord. We use the term "7th" because the note is a 7th above the root.

The labeling of a 7th chord pertains to the type of triad and 7th it contains. For instance, a C major 7 is a C triad with a major seventh (♮7). C7, C minor 7, C half-diminished 7, and C7+5 all have a minor seventh (♭7); however, C7 has a major triad, C minor 7 a minor triad, C half-diminished 7 a diminished triad, and C7+5 an augmented triad. C augmented-major 7 has an augmented triad with a major 7th, and C diminished 7 (also called "fully diminished") has a diminished triad and a diminished, or double-flatted 7th.

Table 6.1 illustrates a helpful method of interpreting 7th chord symbols. Think of a 7th chord symbol as potentially containing four columns of data. The first column is the pitch that serves as the root of the chord. The second column is the type of triad, and the third is the type of 7th. If the two columns duplicate each other, use the label only once, i.e. C major-major 7 becomes C major 7. The fourth column is that which contains the number "7" (or, as we will see later, "9," "11," or "13.") The fifth column in the table indicates the name of the chord. One important rule to remember is that a triad is major unless otherwise indicated, and a seventh is minor unless otherwise indicated. That is why we call C major-minor 7 chord "C7". Note also some of the shorthand that is used. For instance, the symbol for major 7 is "Δ," for minor is " ⁻," for augmented is "+," for half-diminished 7 is "ø," and for fully diminished is " °." Some arrangers use "Δ7" to denote Major 7th chords; however, this is technically redundant, as the triangle is generally thought to signify a Major 7th chord. It is, at times, easier to understand, as there are invariably people from another universe who believe that the triangle means "Major" and not "Major 7". In other words, if there is any doubt, the arranger may wish to stay on the safe side and add the "7".

72

7th Chords and Nashville Numbers

The Nashville system uses 7th chords. The difficulty is differentiating the chord suffix from the chord number. A small superscript number, such as 5^7 represents the suffix. This is also relatively simple to do with a word processing program. Additional suffixes appear as they normally would. Examples of this are: $6^{-7}, 2ø^7, b3Δ^7, 5+^7$. In the Nashville system, a 7 usually follows the Δ. These rules also apply to 6^{th}s, as well as extensions as seen in the following chapter.

Table 6.1 Chord Symbols for 7th Chords

Root	Triad	Type of seventh	(7)	Chord Labels
C	major	major	7	CMaj.7, CΔ
C	major	minor	7	C7
C	minor	minor	7	Cmin. 7, C⁻7
C	diminished	minor	7	Cø, C⁻7b5
C	diminished	diminished	7	C°7
C	minor	major	7	C minor-major 7, C⁻Δ
C	augmented	major	7	C+Maj. 7, C+Δ, CΔ+5, CΔ♯5
C	augmented	minor	7	C+7, C7+5, C7♯5
C	sus4	major	7	CΔsus4, CΔsus
C	sus4	minor	7	C7sus4, C7sus
C	sus2	major	7	CΔsus2
C	sus2	minor	7	C7sus2

Example 6.1 7th Chords

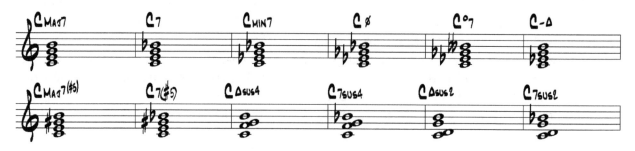

Ear-Training Assignment 6.1: Demonstrate ability to identify all twelve types of 7th chords listed in Example 6.1.

73

7th Chords as Slash Chords

Another way of looking at 7th chords is as slash chords, with a triad over a root, as in Table 6.2. This is especially useful when learning to play them on the piano.

Table 6.2 7th Chords As Slash Chords

Chord	Upper-Structure	Root	Slash Chord
CΔ	E⁻	C	E⁻/C
C7	E°	C	E°/C
C⁻7	E♭	C	E♭/C
Cø	E♭⁻	C	E♭⁻/C
C°7	E♭°	C	E♭°/C
C⁻Δ	E♭+	C	E♭+/C
C+Δ	E	C	E/C
CΔsus2	G	C	G/C
C7sus2	G⁻	C	G⁻/C

Example 6.2 Slash Chords for 7th Chords

There are no simple triad upper-structures for the C+7, CΔsus, and C7sus chords. However, we will cover other types of slash chords in later chapters.

> **Written Assignment 6.1:** Write the 6th and 7th chords in the workbook example in two staves.

7th Chord Piano Voicings

The following examples illustrate the most effective piano voicings for playing 7th chords. The voicings in Example 6.3 are in closed-position, with the root in the left hand and the root, 3rd, 5th and 7th in the right hand. These have a very full sound, as the right hand doubles the root.

Example 6.3 Closed-Position Full 7th Chord Voicings

Note that most of the chords with Major 7ths omit the first inversion. Avoid playing the Major 7th chord with the root on the top. The exception is the CΔsus2, in which the 1/2-step on top produces an interesting effect. In some cases, each voicing of a chord has a distinctive quality. This is certainly true with the C+7 chord, as the second, third and fourth inversions in the right hand produce different note clusters a whole-step apart. In the context of a song, the pianist will typically choose the voicing that is easiest to reach from the chord preceding it. However, the composer may feel that a specific voicing best fits the character of the song.

The second type of chord voicing is the rootless voicing, where the right hand omits the root, illustrated in Example 6.4:

Example 6.4 Rootless 7th Chord Voicings

This example omits the fully-diminished, sus2 and sus4 chords, as they require the full sound induced by the inclusion of the root in the right hand.

The third type of 7th chord voicing consists of only the 3rd and 7th in the right hand. In most 7th chords, the notes which define the chord quality are the 3rd and 7th. This is especially true with the Dominant 7th chord. In traditional theory, the 5 chord is often a dominant 7th chord. Furthermore, in the traditional dominant-to-tonic chord progression (5⁷-1) the 3rd of the 5⁷ chord moves up 1/2-step to the root of the 1 chord, and the 7th of the 5 chord moves down 1/2-step to the 3rd of the 1 chord. This strong voice-leading tendency is one of the defining aspects of the dominant 7th chord.

However, the 5th is the defining element of diminished and augmented chords, and they are not included in this example. Similarly, the 5th is rather important in sus2 and sus4 chords, and those chords are not included as well.

Example 6.5 Rootless 7th Chord Voicings with no 5th

Open-position piano voicings are also very effective for some 7th chords. The *quartal* and *quintal* construction of these voicings produces an "open" quality. A quartal voicing is a chord voicing consisting mostly of notes spaced a fourth apart. Furthermore, a quintal voicing is a chord voicing consisting mostly of notes spaced a fifth apart. Example 6.6 illustrates these voicings.

Example 6.6 Open 7th Chord Voicings

6th Chords

A 6th chord is simply a triad with an added 6th. The added 6th is usually a whole-step above the 5th, as it is in the major scale. In situations where the 6th is 1/2 step above the natural 5th, write the chord in this nomenclature C(♭6). Pop music rarely uses this type of chord. The use of parentheses is important, or the musician will play a C♭ triad with an added 6th. Chord symbol notation for 6th chords is relatively simple. For instance, notate a C major triad with an added sixth as a C6, and a C minor triad with an added 6th as Cminor6, Cmin6, Cmi6, or C-6.

Example 6.7 6th Chords

An additional type of 6th chord is the 6/9 chord. This type of chord consists of a major or minor triad with an added 6th as well as an added 9th (natural 2nd.) The term 9th is used rather than 6th, because most pianists will voice the note above the 6th. The use of the term 9th will be discussed further in the next chapter. Similar to the 6th, the 9th is a whole-step above the root. The 6/9 and minor 6/9 chords are illustrated in Example 6.8:

Example 6.8 6/9 chords

As illustrated above, the preferred chord symbol places the 6 above the 9. However, this cannot be easily done on a computer keyboard, so the designation "6/9" is acceptable as well.

The standard piano voicings for 6th and 6/9 chords include the root or 9th on top in the right hand. This is not to imply that any other voicings are unacceptable; however, the voicing with the root or 9th on top, as illustrated in Example 6.9, is the most commonly used.

Example 6.9 6th and 6/9 Chord Piano Voicings

The 6/9 voicings depicted above posses an "open" quality when played, due to the quartal nature of the right-hand voicing. Occasionally, published pop sheet music will use the chord symbols "Maj6" or "Maj6/9". However, it should be obvious that the use of the word "major" is not required with 6th chords.

> **Keyboard Assignment 6.3:** Learn to play the voicings in Example 6.9, in all keys.

Review 3: The Dominant 7th Chord in Authentic Cadences

The 5[7] to 1 cadence contains two powerful leading tones, so named because they have a strong tendency to move up or down by a half step. The third of the 5[7] chord leads up by a minor 2nd to the root of the 1 chord, and the 7th of the 5[7] chord leads down by a minor 2nd to the 3rd of the 1 chord (Example 6.10.)

Example 6.10 Leading Tone Movement in the 5^7-1 Cadence

6th and 7th Chords in Pop Chord Progressions

Popular music uses 6th and 7th chords in a variety of different ways. Dominant 7th chords still frequently fulfill dominant or secondary dominant chord functions, but they function in other ways as well. Even early pop styles use augmented dominant 7th as dominant chords as well. Quite frequently, the big band jazz era used 6th chords, which carried into early rock and roll. However, in jazz, the major 7th chord replaced the 6th chord by the 1950's. Mainstream pop music did not use the major 7th chord until the late 1960's. In lieu of a simple triad, use 6th and major 7th chords to fulfill a 1 or 4 chord function. Minor 7th and half-diminished 7th chords usually fulfill a 2m or 2° function, and minor 7th chords can replace 1m chords in minor keys.

In most modern jazz styles, as well as some blues styles, use 7th chords almost exclusively, and you will rarely find simple triads, except in slash chords.

The 1-$1\triangle^7$-1^7-1^6 Progression and Variants

In a progression, use 6th and 7th chords to provide an ascending or descending note movement, usually in minor or major 2nds. Example 6.11 illustrates two progressions containing a descending line.

Example 6.11 1-$1\triangle^7$-1^7-1^6 and 1-$1\triangle^7$-1^7-6^7 Progressions

The top notes of the right-hand voicings indicate the descending line. Note that both progressions contain the same 1/2-step note movement: C-B-B♭-A. Repetition of the first progression may occur several times. However, the 6^7 at the end of the second progression will typically lead to a new chord, most likely a 2 chord.

79

Example 6.12 illustrates two chord progressions using an ascending line.

Example 6.12 $1\text{-}1\text{+}\text{-}1^6\text{-}1\text{+}$ and $1\text{-}1^6\text{-}1\Delta^7\text{-}1^6$ Progressions

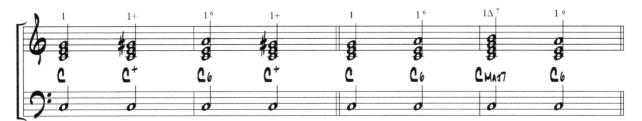

Once again, the line is in the top note of the right hand. In both cases, the line ascends then descends to the last note. Both of these progressions will typically repeat several times. Both of the above examples illustrate techniques of adding a bit of a melodic element to a chord progression, using chord symbols.

2m-5-1 Progressions

The 2m-5-1 is one of the most common chord progressions found in jazz, as well as in Western music as a whole. In jazz, it is a "II-V-I" but for the sake of convenience, we will simply refer to it as the 2-5-1. Use of the 2-5-1 does not follow the same strict rules found in traditional music theory. The term 2-5-1 as used in jazz refers to chord relationships rather than strict key relationships. Many jazz standards, if analyzed with Roman or Nashville numbers, tend to modulate every two to four measures, usually returning to the original key near the end of the song, or at the end of each section. However, in jazz, it is not standard practice to indicate a new key signature every time this occurs. Furthermore, classical theorists may even characterize some of these "modulations" as secondary sub-dominants and dominants. For this reason, Nashville numbers do not work as well with jazz.

7th chords dominate the 2-5-1 progression in jazz. Example 6.13 illustrates a major and minor 2-5-1 progression commonly used in jazz.

Example 6.13 Major and Minor 2-5-1 Progressions

Note that the 1 chord in the major 2-5-1 is a major 7th chord, and the 1 chord in the minor 2-5-1 is a minor 7th chord. Note that the 2 chord in the minor progression is a half-diminished 7th chord. Jazz and pop styles use the 2-5-1 progressions in a variety of ways. They provide an easy transition to another chord, or as turnaround progressions. In some jazz standards, 2-5-1 progressions make up the entire song.

In this context, they suggest a movement through a number of key centers. Example 6.14 contains a succession of 2-5-1 chords that seem to modulate from C to Bb to Ab.

Example 6.14 Jazz 2-5-1 Progression

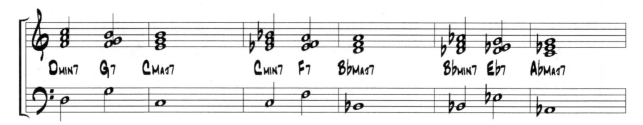

This type of progression is typical in jazz, where a 1 chord becomes the 2m chord for the next key center.

Jazz compositions that encompass a 2-5 without a clear I chord are prevalent. In the majority of cases, the root movement will be the same, as illustrated in Example 6.15.

Example 6.15 2-5 Progressions

In measures 1 and 2, the 5^7 chord leads to the next $2m^7$, rather than to a $1\Delta^7$; however, the root movement is still down a 5th. At times, the 5^7 might lead to another chord, usually a major 2nd up or a minor 2nd down. This breaks all the rules of traditional harmony, but it works.

Below is a brief list of some well-known Jazz standards that encompass many 2-5-1 progressions.

Examples of Jazz Standards Using 2-5-1 progressions:

e *All The Things You Are* – Jerome Kern/Oscar Hammerstein II
e *Autumn Leaves* – Joseph Kosma/Jacques Prevert/Johnny Mercer
e *How High the Moon* – Morgan Lewis/Nancy Hamilton
e *I've Got You Under My Skin* – Cole Porter
e *Just Friends* – John Klenner/Samuel H. Lewis
e *Our Love is Here To Stay* – George and Ira Gershwin
e *Satin Doll* – Duke Ellington/Billy Strayhorn/Johnny Mercer

Keyboard Assignment 6.4: Learn to play the major 2-5-1 progression in Example 6.13 in all keys.

1-6-2-5 Progressions with 7th Chords

The use of the 1-6-2-5 progression has proliferated over the years. Often a composer will add a bit of harmonic interest by using all 7th chords, as in Example 6.16.

Example 6.16 1^6-$6m^7$-$2m^7$-5^7 Progression

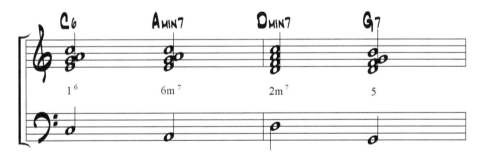

Although the progression in Example 6.16 is rendered a bit more interesting using 7th chords, it still can be a bit mundane. As the root movements between the 6, 2, and 5 chord are all in 4ths, composers and musicians realized that all three of those chords could be dominant 7th chords, thus making the progression more harmonically interesting (Example 6.17)

Example 6.17 1^6-6^7-2^7-5^7 Progression

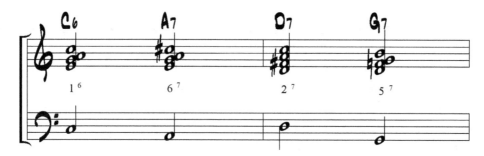

Both of the above progressions are especially useful as turnarounds, and many songs (such as Gershwin's *I've Got Rhythm*) feature these progressions prominently.

7th Chords and the 12-Bar Blues

Dominant 7th chords make up many variations of 12-bar blues Of course, such use of the dominant 7th chord would break the rules of traditional music theory, in which only the 5 chord in the key would be a dominant 7th. However, this serves the blues well, in that there is a constant "leading-tone" type of half-step movement between the thirds and sevenths of each chord, as illustrated in the F blues progression in Example 6.18.

Example 6.18 12-Bar Blues Progression in F

Note the use of chord substitutions in this example. For instance, measure 4 would traditionally contain only an F7. Instead, use a 2-5 in Bb to provide a stronger harmonic movement toward the Bb7 chord in measure 5. A 1^7-6^7-2^7-5^7 progression follows in measures 7-10, with chromatic passing chords leading from the F7 to the D7. The last two measures of the form contain a classic turnaround progression, leading back to the 1 chord at the repeat.

6th and 7th chords in Slash Chords

Do not confuse this section with the section above regarding 7th chords *as* slash chords. Use 6th and 7th chords as the top chord in chord-over-bass-note slash chords. The most obvious example of this is triad-over-bass-note slash chords that form 7th chords with the 7th in the bass, such as 1/7 (Major 7th,) 1/b7 (Dominant 7th,) 1m/b7 (minor 7th,) 1/6 (6th,) and 1m/6 (minor 6th.) Label any of those chords as 6th or 7th chords, if the composer wishes to emphasize that aspect of the chord. Thus, a C/B can be called a Cmaj7/B, a C/Bb can be called a C7/Bb, and so on. Of course, the composer should only use this if they absolutely want the bass note doubled in the chord.

Use 6th and 7th in slash chords in virtually the same ways as triads, as inversions or as passing chords for a bass line. A 5^7/3 leading to a 1 chord is especially effective, with the third of the 5 chord moving up to the root of the 1 chord. Use any type of chord-over-bass-note configuration for 6th and 7th chords. Be aware that certain bass notes may alter the sound of a slash chord, making it sound like another chord. Example 6.19 illustrates one such chord, a C6/A.

Example 6.19 C6/A

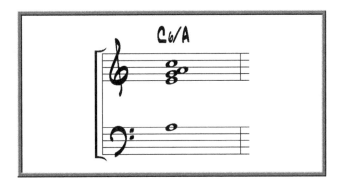

When played on the piano, this chord sounds more like an A minor 7 than a C6 because it contains all the elements of that chord. In fact, if a composer wished to use such a slash chord, and liked the sound of it, it would be wise to simply call it an Amin7, rather than a C6/A. It is always easier to read a root-position chord symbol than a slash chord. Consequently, when using slash chords, it is a good idea to analyze them and make sure that there is not a simpler chord symbol. In fact, this is true even with triad slash chords. We have already discussed how an Emin/C is actually a Cmaj7 chord. The only reason to use Emin/C rather than Cmaj7 is to ensure that the right hand plays E minor and that the left hand plays the C.

Jazz and Blues Song Forms

American popular music song forms have evolved greatly in the last century. Early American musical forms, such as the blues, folk music, and traditional jazz, consisted of repeating 12-, 16-, and 32-bar forms. Past and present uses of the terms "verse" and "chorus" have different meanings. This section explains how the song forms of the past, influence the forms, which are still in use today.

12-Bar Blues Form

The 12-bar blues simply repeats the 12-bar form many times. Composition of the 8-bar and 16-bar versions of the blues is the same. At some point, blues artists found they could break the monotony of a 12-bar blues with a "stop-time" section. In a stop-time section, play the 1 chord only on the first beat of the first three measures of the form. In the fourth measure, the 1 chord plays throughout measure, and the bass "walks up" to the 4 chord (Example 6.20.)

Example 6.20 Stop-Time Section

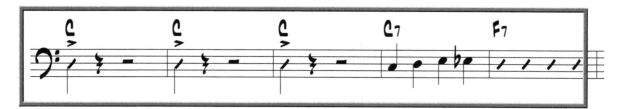

The vocalist continues singing during the rests, as well as the walk-up. There are many variations of stop-time choruses in the 12-bar blues, but this type is most common usage today.

Base the analysis of a blues composition on the melody, lyrics and the presence of stop-time sections. In other words, one might think that the form of a blues would simply be labeled A A A…. However, there is often a section containing a different melody or a repeated set of lyrics, which would indicate the "Chorus" of the song. A stop-time section may be the chorus or a bridge.

Note that there is another usage of the word *chorus* in blues and jazz practice. For instance, a *chorus* in the blues indicates one time through the 12-bar form. Similarly, a *chorus* in jazz improvisation indicates one time through the entire form of the song, even if the song form is 32 measures. When a jazz musician wishes to solo over two choruses of a 32-bar form, he/she will play a 64-bar solo.

Jazz and Broadway Standards

Broadway musicals and *Tin Pan Alley* gave us many popular songs, which today are beloved jazz standards. Broadway and jazz composers constructed these songs in a different manner; our composers today still use these forms.

The main part of the song is typically in a 32-bar form, with four 8-measure sections, although 64 bars with four 16-measure sections is possible as well. The most common configurations of these sections are A-A-B-A, A–B–A–B, or A–B–A–C. Some of these forms may consist of modified repeated A or B sections, such as A-A^1-B-A, A-A^1-B-A^2, A-B-A^1-B^1 or A-B-A-B^1, or A-B-A^1-C. In these cases, the repeated section is modified so that the melody and/or chord progression has been altered somewhat. The superscript numbers after the section letter indicate that the repeated section is different from one or more of the others. Some standards have more than four sections, and a few even have four completely different sections (A-B-C-D,) but these are rare.

When sung, the song is sometimes in a *strophic* form, with the 32-bar form repeated several times, with new lyrics at each repeat. In instrumental jazz, however, the melody is usually played one time through, with several choruses of improvised solos, followed by a repeat of either the entire melody or the last 16 measures. In jazz terminology, we call this 32-bar form with the melody the *head*. The term is a reference to a form of any length; it simply means that the band or soloist will play the melody one time through. For example, the bandleader on a gig may say: "Let's play one time through the head, take 3 choruses of solo, then play the head one more time."

Many Broadway songs also include a different type of *verse*, which precedes the 32-bar form. This type of verse is similar to a "recitative" in opera, in that it sets the scene or leads up to the song. Verses of this type are often *through-composed*, although some can be strophic. The lyrics are usually more important than the melody, and the melody and chord progression are typically different from the rest of the song. The rhythm of the melody and lyrics is often very conversational in style. The accompaniment may be *rubato* or in time, and usually only consists of piano or guitar, playing each chord only once. In most cases, the drums and bass do not enter until the last several measures of the verse.

In analysis of a Jazz standard or Broadway song that follows this format, it may be easiest to treat the verse as an intro, labeling it "intro (verse)".

"Rhythm" Changes

"Rhythm" Changes, the chord changes to the famous Gershwin composition "I Got Rhythm," comprise a standard 32-bar chord progression frequently found in jazz. Example 6.21 illustrates one of the standard incarnations of rhythm changes, in C. Artists still use this form as pictured although many tend to use chord substitutions. Rhythm changes are the basis of a number of standard jazz compositions. Rhythm Changes has four 8-measure sections, and the form is A-A-B-A.

Example 6.21 Rhythm Changes

Written Assignment 6.3: Analyze the form of two jazz standards in the Real Book.
Written Assignment 6.4: Compose a song using one of the song forms discussed in this section. Demonstrate good melodic construction, as well as accurate use of the form.

Examples of Jazz/Broadway Standard Song Forms

A-A-B-A (Including Rhythm Changes), A-A^1-B-A, A-A^1-B-A^2

All The Things You Are – Jerome Kern/Oscar Hammerstein II
Don't Get Around Much Anymore – Duke Ellington/Bob Russell
Georgia On My Mind – Hoagy Carmichael/Stuart Gorrell
I Get a Kick Out of You – Cole Porter
I Got Rhythm – George and Ira Gershwin
I'm Beginning to See the Light – Harry James/Duke Ellington/Johnny Hodges/Don George
I've Got The World on a String – Harold Arlen/Ted Koehler
Let It Snow! Let It Snow! Let It Snow! – Jule Styne/Sammy Cahn
Love and Marriage – Jimmy Van Heusen/Sammy Cahn
Misty – Erroll Garner/Johnny Burke
On the Sunny Side of the Street – Jimmy McHugh/Dorothy Fields
Over The Rainbow – Harold Arlen/E.Y. Harburg
Round Midnight – Cootie Williams/Thelonious Monk/Bernie Hanighen
Satin Doll – Duke Ellington/Billy Strayhorn/Johnny Mercer
Take The "A" Train – Billy Strayhorn/Lee Gaines
They Can't Take That Away From Me – George and Ira Gershwin
The Way You Look Tonight – Jerome Kern/Dorothy Fields

A-B-A-B, A-B-A^1-B^1, A-B-A-B^1

Fly Me to the Moon – Bart Howard
How High The Moon – Morgan Lewis/Nancy Hamilton
I Thought About You – Jimmy Van Heusen/Johnny Mercer
Just Friends – John Klenner/Samuel H. Lewis
Our Love is Here To Stay – George and Ira Gershwin
There Will Never Be Another You – Harry Warren/Mack Gordon
Unforgettable – Irving Gordon

A-B-A-C, A-B-A^1-C

All Of Me – Gerald Marks/Seymour Simons
The More I See You – Harry Warren/Mack Gordon
My Romance – Richard Rodgers/Lorenz Hart
Stardust – Hoagy Carmichael/Mitchell Parish
Young At Heart –Johnny Richards/Carolyn Leigh

It can be difficult to differentiate between an A-B-A-B1 form and an A-B-A-C form. The song *Young At Heart*, listed under the A-B-A-C column, is one such instance. The fourth section begins like the first B section, but the last half of the section is radically different. Arguably, either category would apply in this case.

Checklist of Assignments for Chapter 6

- ✓ **Ear-Training Assignment 6.1:** Demonstrate ability to identify all twelve types of 7th chords listed in Example 6.1.
- ✓ **Written Assignment 6.1:** Write out the 6th and 7th chords, in two staves with the root in the bass clef.
- ✓ **Keyboard Assignment 6.1:** Learn to play at least one of the voicings for dominant 7th, Major 7th, minor 7th, and half-diminished 7th chords, in all keys.
- ✓ **Keyboard Assignment 6.2:** Learn to play one of the voicings of each of the remaining 7th chords listed above, with C as the root.
- ✓ **Keyboard Assignment 6.3:** Learn to play the voicings in Example 6.9, in all keys.
- ✓ **Keyboard Assignment 6.4:** Learn to play the major 2-5-1 progression in Example 6.13 in all keys.
- ✓ **Written Assignment 6.2:** Compose a chord progression of at least 16 measures, at least one chord per measure. At least eight of the chords must be 6th and 7th chords.
- ✓ **Written Assignment 6.3:** Analyze the form of two jazz standards in the Real Book or some other source.
- ✓ **Written Assignment 6.4:** Compose a song using one of the song forms discussed in this section. Demonstrate good melodic construction, as well as accurate use of the form.

7

EXTENSIONS

In jazz and pop music, the term *Extensions* refers to notes found in a chord in addition to the root, third, fifth and seventh. These extensions are known as the 9th (or 2nd) 11th (or 4th) and 13th (or 6th.) Extensions typically extend beyond the seventh of a chord, thus the name. Example 7.1 illustrates the different ways to interpret a seventh chord with extensions. The first is as a seven-note chord stacked in thirds, the second as an arpeggio, and the third within the context of a scale.

Example 7.1 Seventh Chord with Extensions

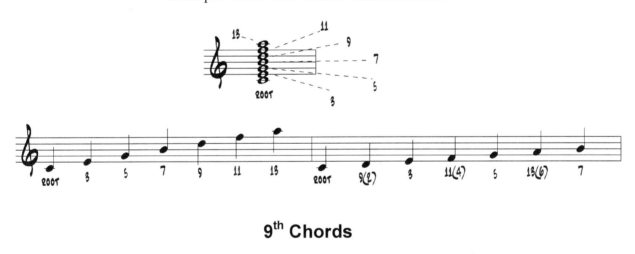

9th Chords

There is a simple method for labeling chords with extensions. The absence or presence of a 7th is the crucial ingredient for determining which chord symbol to use. Before we explain further, look at Example 7.2.

Example 7.2 Chord Symbols with Extensions

Note that the first two chords contain 7^{th}s, while the second two do not. Use C(add2) when the 9th is just above the root in the right hand (measure 3,) and C(add9) when the 9th is in the octave above. In common practice, the two labels are interchangeable, and can describe either voicing. However, it is suggested that "add2" be used whenever the composer wishes the 9th to be voiced between the root and 3rd, as this is how it will often be interpreted.

As with the 7th chords in the previous chapter, it may help to think of the elements of an extended chord as belonging to different categories. In this case, the three categories are:
1. Type of triad,
2. Presence or absence of a 7th, and the type of 7th, and
3. Type of extension.

Table 7.1 illustrates these categories, using major and minor chords with added 9^{th}s:

Table 7.1 Categories in Chords with Extensions

Triad	7th	Extension	Chord Symbol
major	major	9	Cmaj9
major	minor	9	C9
major	----	9 (2)	C(add2), C(add9)
minor	minor	9	Cmin9
minor	----	9	Cmin(add2), Cmin(add9)

It should be obvious by now that extended chords follow rules similar to those used with 7th chords. The chord symbol for a 7th chord with an added 9th will be the almost the same, but the "7" in the symbol is replaced by a "9," because it is implied that the chord contains a 7th. On the other hand, if the chord does not contain a 7th but does contain a 9th, use the symbol for the base triad plus "add2" or "add9". The use of parentheses around the "add2" and "add9" is optional, and completely up to the individual. An additional useful symbol for a C triad with an added 9th is C2. Composers do not use this symbol as frequently as the add2 or add9.

The reader also may have noticed that the Table 7.1 does not indicate the kind of 9th that is in the chord. The assumption is that it is a major 9th, or a major 2nd above the root. If a chord has a different type of 9th, there are other ways to indicate it, which we will discuss in a later chapter.

Use of add2 and add9 Chords in Pop Music

Many songwriters use Add 2 chords quite frequently in pop music, especially in compositions that feature keyboard. The most common type of voicing is one in which the 9th is placed between the root and 3rd, forming a cluster of whole-steps. In order to achieve this effect, the right-hand voicing must be in root position or second inversion, as illustrated in Example 7.3:

91

Example 7.3 Common Piano Voicings for Add2 chords

Many writers used this type of piano voicing in the piano-based pop ballads of the 1970's and '80's.

Keyboard Assignment 7.1: Learn to play the add2 piano voicings in Example 7.3 in all keys.
Ear-Training Assignment 7.1: Practice identifying all of the 9th and add9 chords.
Written Assignment 7.1: Write out the 9th chords on two staves with the root in the bass clef.

9th Chord Voicings

When playing 9th chords on the piano, it is sometimes helpful to think of them as slash chords, with a 7th chord in the right hand over a bass note in the left hand. This works for six different 9th chords, as illustrated in Example 7.4:

Example 7.4 9th Slash Chord Piano Voicings

These are probably the best voicings for 9th chords, although it is also possible to use a rootless voicing in the right hand with the 9th below the 3rd. Example 7.5 illustrates additional piano voicings for the 9th chords most commonly used in pop music.

Example 7.5 Additional 9th Chord Piano Voicings

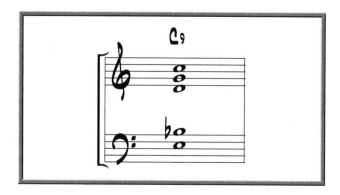

There is also an excellent rootless quartal voicing for use in a band situation when there is a bass player playing the root. Example 7.6 illustrates this voicing.

Example 7.6 Rootless 9th Chord Piano Voicing

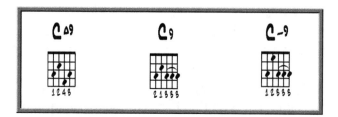

So as not to leave the guitarists out, Example 7.7 illustrates some common 9th chord voicings for guitar.

Example 7.7 9th Chord Voicings for Guitar

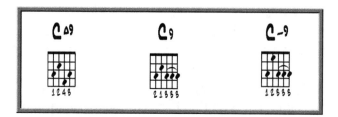

93

11th and 13th Chords

For instance, the chord depicted in example 7.1, which is a C major 7 with an added 9th, 11th, and 13th, may be labeled as illustrated in Figure 6.1.

CΔ	CΔ 9 11 13 ♭11 ♭13	CΔ♭9

Figure 7.1 Chord Symbols for C Major 7 with an Added 9th, 11th, and 13th

The first chord name, CΔ13, is the easiest to use, in that it usually implies that there is a 7th, 9th and 11th in the chord as well. If a CΔ chord with only an added 9th were preferable, we would simply call it CΔ9. It is interesting to note that in jazz, the ♮11th is not usually used in a chord with a major 3rd, such as CΔ13 or C13. This is because the ♮11 or ♮4 is a half step away from the ♮3, and this produces an undesirable dissonance. In jazz, composers refer to the ♮4 in a chord with a major 3rd as the *Avoid Tone* or *Avoid Note*. Furthermore, many jazz musicians will interpret a C11 chord as a C9sus. In pop music, however, you can use the ♮11 in conjunction with the ♮3.

One must also be careful not to confuse the chord CΔ13 with the chord C6. C6 implies that a major triad incorporates the sixth degree but there is no 7th. Usually the numbers 9, 11 and 13 imply that the chord includes a 7th. Label chords consisting of triads with added extensions with the numbers 2, 4 and 6, or add9, add11, add13. The exception to this rule is the 6/9 chord, which has no 7th. Table 7.2 illustrates the seventh chords and triads with extensions.

Table 7.2 Extensions

Triad	7th Chord	9th	11th	13th
----	CΔ	CΔ9	CΔ11	CΔ13
----	C7	C9	C11	C13
----	C-7	C⁻9	C⁻11	C⁻13
C	----	C2 Cadd2 Cadd9	Cadd4 Cadd11	C6 C6/9
C-	----	C⁻2 C⁻add2 C⁻add9	C⁻add4 C⁻add11	C⁻6 C⁻6/9
----	Cø	Cø9 C⁻9♭5	Cø11 C⁻11♭5	Cø13 C⁻13♭5
----	C°7	C°9	C°11	----
----	C⁻Δ	C⁻Δ9	C⁻Δ11	C⁻Δ13
----	CΔ+5	CΔ9+5	----	----
----	C7+5	C9+5	----	----
C+	----	C2+5 C+add2 C+add9	----	----
----	CΔsus4	CΔ9sus4	----	CΔ13sus4
----	C7sus4	C9sus4	----	C13sus4
Csus4	----	C2sus4 Csus4(add9)	----	C6sus4
----	CΔsus2	----	CΔ11sus2	CΔ13sus2
----	C7sus2	----	C11sus2	C13sus2
Csus2	----	----	Csus2add4 Csus2add11	C6sus2

The first two columns indicate whether a triad or 7th chord build the basis for the extension. The third, fourth and fifth columns illustrate the correct chord symbol to use if the chord includes a 9th, 11th or 13th. Remember that 11th chords imply the inclusion of the 9th, and 13th chords imply the inclusion of the 9th and 11th. If the intent of the composer is the use of a C13 with no 9th or 11th, the best label for the chord may be C7add13. However, not all musicians will automatically add the 9th and 11th in a 13th chord. It is often a matter of personal playing style, as well as the number of voicings the pianist or guitarist knows. It is also occasionally more difficult for a guitarist to play more than one extension in a chord.

Example 7.8 illustrates the three common 11th chord piano voicings.

Example 7.8 11th Chord Piano Voicings

Note that in the first and third measures, the one must place the 11th above the root, and there is no 9th. These are common pop voicings, especially for 11th chords with a natural 3rd. In fact, the major 7th or minor 9th that would result when separating the natural 3rd and natural 11th can be rather harsh. In the minor 11th chord, however, this is not an issue, and the guitar-like voicing in measure 2 is very effective.

There are also several very useful voicings for dominant and major 13th chords, including several rootless quartal voicings, as illustrated in Example 7.9.

Example 7.9 13th Chord Piano Voicings

Example 7.10 illustrates several examples of 11th and 13th chord guitar voicings:

Example 7.10 Guitar Voicings for 11th and 13th Chords

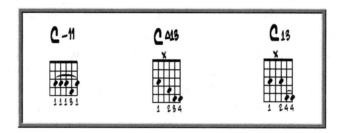

Keyboard Assignment 7.2: Learn the 2-5-1 patterns with extensions in Example 7.11 in all keys.

Example 7.11 2-5-1 Patterns With Extensions

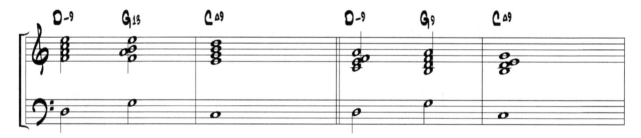

"Altered" Extensions

An *altered extension* is a flatted or sharped extension. How does one know when there is a flatted or sharped extension? When we say that an extension is in it's "natural" form, the model we use is the major scale. In the major scale, the 9th is a whole-step above the root, the 11th is a perfect 4th above the root, and the 13th is a major 6th above the root (or a minor 3rd below the root.) Thus, if the 9th is a half step above the root, we call it a ♭9, and if the 11th is a tritone above the root, we label it a ♯11.

In a chord symbol with an altered extension, the 7th or the highest unaltered extension will be listed first, followed by the altered extension(s). For instance, label a C7 chord with a ♯9 (D♯) as C7♯9 or C7(♯9). If labeled merely as C♯9, the musician would play a C♯7 chord with an added 9th. Similarly, a C7 chord with a natural 9 and ♯11 would be C9♯11, and a C7 chord with a natural 13 and a ♯11 would be C13♯11.

Perhaps the most famous example of the use of altered extensions is the E7♯9 chord used by Jimi Hendrix in the song *Purple Haze* (Example 7.12.)

97

Example 7.12 Dominant 7#9 Chord

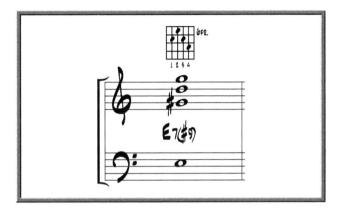

This chord, sometimes known as the "Jimi Hendrix Chord", is very powerful due to the tension between the ♯9 (which is basically an enharmonic respelling of the minor 3rd) and the natural 3rd. The minor blues scale is very effective for writing melodies or soloing over this type of chord.

The ♯11 is another extension used frequently, especially in major 7th and dominant 7th chords. Utilize it to solve the problem of the 1/2-step clash between the natural 3rd and natural 11th. Common chord symbols for chords with sharp 11's are: Cmaj7♯11, Cmaj9♯11, Cmaj13♯11, C7♯11, C9♯11, and C13♯11.

An altered dominant 7th chord is one in which all of the extensions are altered, and the chord symbol looks like this: C7alt. The altered chord contains a ♭9, ♯9, ♯11, and ♭13, and no 5th. In practice, the pianist or guitarist will play either the ♭9 or ♯9. They are rarely played together in a chord. We will explore the theory behind altered extensions in a later chapter.

(Note: A more complete listing of guitar voicings is included at the end of this book, in the section entitled Chord Voicings for Guitar. 6th and 7th chords, as well as chords covered in later chapters, are also included.)

Ear-Training Assignment 7.2: Practice identifying all the 11th and 13th chords, as well as the Dominant 7#9 chord.
Written Assignment 7.2: Write out the following extended chords on two staves with the root in the bass clef.

Harmonizing Melodies Using 6th, 7th, and Extended Chords

6th, 7th, and extended chords give the composer more options in harmonizing a melody. If it seems a specific chord should occur in a certain place, but the melody is not a chord tone, try using a 7th chord or extended chord, or even a chord with altered extensions, which includes the melody note. A melody is not required to reside within the primary chord tones. Be aware, however, that the melody may sound more exotic or "jazzy".

Checklist of Assignments for Chapter 7

✓ **Keyboard Assignment 7.1:** Learn to play the add2 piano voicings in Example 7.3 in all keys.

✓ **Ear-Training Assignment 7.1:** Practice identifying the 9th and add9 chords.

✓ **Written Assignment 7.1:** Write out the following 9th chords on two staves with the root in the bass clef.

✓ **Keyboard Assignment 7.2:** Learn the 2-5-1 patterns with extensions in Example 6.11 below, in all keys.

✓ **Ear-Training Assignment 7.2:** Practice identifying the 11th and 13th chords, as well as the Dominant 7#9 chord.

✓ **Written Assignment 7.2:** Write out the extended chords on two staves with the root in the bass clef.

8

CHORD-SCALE THEORY, AND MODES OF THE

MAJOR SCALE

Chord-Scale Theory is the process of building a chord from the notes of a scale or mode. It is an important and useful tool for the composer. Knowledge of chord scales allows composers to analyze a melody and determine which chords will most easily fit the melodic line. The reverse is true as well, for composers can write a chord progression, and then compose a melody using the appropriate chord scales.

Additionally, most modern musicians utilize chord-scale theory in their improvisations. Back in the 1930's, musicians were more apt to arpeggiate the notes of a chord in their improvisations than think of them as scale-like lines or melodic constructs, but that began to change in the 1940's. In effect, they transposed the extensions down an octave so that they were situated next to the root, 3rd, 5th and 7th, thus forming a scale.

Modes of the Major Scale

Modes are scales constructed from each degree of a scale, in this case, the major scale. The ancient Greeks originally devised the names assigned to each mode. They believed that each mode elicited a different mood response from the listener (the word "mood" is derived from the word "mode.") Of course, the modern modes may bear little resemblance to those of the ancient Greeks, for they had no method of exact musical notation. The modes in their present form were derived from those used by the Roman Catholic Church during the Middle Ages. Example 8.1 below illustrates the modes of the major scale, and some of the chords associated with each mode.

Example 8.1 Modes of Major

Order of Whole Steps and Half Steps

The reader should be aware of the order of whole steps and half steps in the major scale and its modes. Example 8.2 pictures a two-octave C major scale.

Example 8.2 Whole Steps and Half Steps in a Two-Octave Major Scale

(w=whole step   h=half step)

Note that two whole steps on one side and three whole steps on the other separate the half steps. Although this spacing remains the same in each of the modes, the physical order of the spacing in relationship to the root of the mode will change. In other words, it is important to remember where the half steps are in each of the modes. For instance, in Lydian, the half steps are between the 4th and 5th degree and the 7th and root. In Mixolydian, they are between the 3rd and 4th degree, and the 6th and 7th degree. Example 8.3 illustrates the location of whole steps and half steps in the modes.

Example 8.3 Whole Steps and Half Steps in the Modes of Major

(w=whole step   h=half step)

Chord Scales for the Modes of Major

Example 8.1 above illustrated some 7th and extended chords associated with the modes of major. In truth, most of the chords used in pop music are derived from the chord scales of the major modes. This includes triads, 6th chords, 7th chords, chords with added extensions, extended chords, and even several slash chords. Table 8.1 illustrates the chord scales for the modes of major:

Table 8.1 Chord Scales for the Modes of Major

Mode	Triad	Triad Chord Symbol	7th Chord	7th Chord Symbols	Extensions	Extended Chord Symbols	Added Extension, Sus2, Slash Chord Symbols
Ionian	Major	C Csus	Major 7	CΔ CΔsus CΔsus2	♮9 ♮11 ♮13	CΔ9 CΔ11 CΔ13 CΔ9sus CΔ13sus	C6 C2 Cadd9 Cadd11 Csus2 C6/9
Dorian	Minor	D⁻	Minor 7	C-7	♮9 ♮11 ♮13	D⁻9 D⁻11 D⁻13	D⁻6 D⁻add9 D⁻add11
Phrygian	Minor, ♭2/1	E⁻ F/E	Minor 7, ♭2 Major 7/1	E-7 FΔ/E	♮11	FΔ9/E	E⁻add11 F/E
Lydian	Major	F	Major 7	FΔ FΔsus2	♮9 #11 ♮13	FΔ9 FΔ9#11 FΔ13#11 FΔ7#11	F6 F2 Fadd9 Fsus2 F6/9 G/F
Mixolydian	Major	G Gsus	Dominant 7	G7 G7sus G7sus2	♮9 ♮11 ♮13	G9 G11 G13 G9sus G13sus	G6 G2 Gadd9 Gadd11 Gsus2 F/G FΔ/G
Aeolian	Minor	A⁻	Minor 7	A-7	♮9 ♮11 ♭13	A⁻9 A⁻11 A⁻11♭13 A-7♭13	A⁻add9 A⁻add11 FΔ/A
Locrian	Diminished	B°	Half-diminished 7	Bᵼ Bᵼ7 B-7♭5	♭9 ♮11 ♭13	Bᵼ7♭9 Bᵼ11♭9 Bᵼ11♭9♭13	–

As evidenced by Table 8.1 above, the modes of major cover a large number of chords. The point to remember is to harmonize a modal melody with any of the chords associated with that particular mode. We will begin by comparing and contrasting similar modes.

Ionian and Lydian

The Ionian and Lydian modes are similar in the type of chords they are associated with: Major 7th chords. The Lydian mode is preferred in jazz with a major 7th chord, because of the ♯11. This eliminates the half step between the ♭3rd of the chord and the ♮4th, which is considered undesirable. The use of the Lydian mode is quite frequent in jazz, while the use of the Ionian mode is in pop music styles.

Use a sus4 chord with Ionian, but not with Lydian. However, either mode can use a sus2 chord with equal effectiveness. The G/F chord constructed from F Lydian sounds very Lydian, because it features the ♯11 prominently (as the 3rd of the G major triad.) Think of this as a 2/1 chord, or a major triad a whole step up from the bass note. Technically this is a 5/4 chord; however, since we are talking about composing a melody using a mode, the root of the mode is actually 1. Therefore, it is proper to call it a 2/1 chord. The ♯11 in Lydian lends it a more exotic sound than Ionian mode.

Dorian and Aeolian

The Dorian mode is most often used on a minor 7th chord in jazz, because the ♯13th provides stronger melodic movement up to the 7th of the chord. The use of the Aeolian mode is often in other pop music styles, as well as some forms of modal jazz. Use a minor 6th chord with Dorian, but not with Aeolian. However, the FΔ/A slash chord constructed from Aeolian is an A minor triad with a flatted 6th. There is infrequent use of the A-7♭13 chord.

Phrygian and Locrian

The Phrygian and Locrian modes look similar at first glance, perhaps due to the ♭9. However, they are very different in function.

Use the Locrian mode with the half-diminished chord. Most jazz composers and musicians, however, feel the ♭9 and ♭13 also produce a less-than-desirable dissonance against the root and 5th of the chord, as well as a weakened upward movement to the next available chord tone. In addition, many times a jazz pianist may play a ♮9 in a half-diminished chord. Other scales are useful for this type of chord, which we will examine in a later chapter.

The use of the Phrygian mode is different. Use of a minor 7th chord with Phrygian is acceptable usually without extensions. The ♭9 does not sound very pleasant with a minor 7th chord. The only usable extension is the natural 11th. In order to avoid the 9th, it would be best to use E‾add11 rather than E‾11. However, another chord used with this mode is a slash chord consisting of a major triad with a bass note 1/2-step below the root. For instance, the slash chord based on E Phrygian would be F/E. That is why Table 8.1 lists the triad as ♭2/1, known as the *Phrygian Chord*.

Mixolydian

Almost every popular music style uses Mixolydian. This is the mode most commonly used with the dominant 7th chord, because of the ♯3 and ♭7. The slash chord, F/G, or ♭7/1, is common in pop music. It is essentially a G9sus4 without the 5th. Similarly, FΔ/G is a G13sus. Mixolydian does not use the 6th chord quite as often. 6th chords tend to sound more similar to major 7th chords than dominant 7th chords.

     The chords constructed from the modes are logical if you think about their functions in the key. For instance, one of the standard mode choices for a dominant 7th chord with no altered extensions is the Mixolydian mode. The Mixolydian mode is based on the 5th degree of the scale, and the 5 chord in traditional harmony is a dominant 7th chord.

> **Ear-Training Assignment 8.1:** Demonstrate ability to sing/play and identify all of the modes of major, in all keys from Example 8.1.

Parent Scales

     The key to using the modes of major in a melody or improvised solo is the ability to identify certain modes with certain types of chords. This is a bit more complicated than it sounds, because there are two things to remember: the mode itself and the major key that contains it, or the *Parent Scale*. For instance, the most appropriate mode for use with a G-7 chord would be the Dorian mode built on the pitch "G". Since, the second degree of the major scale builds the basis of the Dorian mode, one would need to find the major key in which G♯ is the second degree. Since the second degree of the major scale is a whole-step above the root, find the answer (which is the key of F major), by going down a whole-step from G.

     Let's try a few more. The preferred mode for use with a B♭7 chord would be the Mixolydian mode starting on the pitch B♭. Mixolydian is the fifth mode of major, so one would go down a perfect 5th, and come up with the E♭ major scale. One might be tempted to use the C major scale for a CΔ chord, and this is perfectly acceptable, but your solo will be more interesting if you use a Lydian mode built on the pitch C. Lydian is the 4th mode of the major scale, so find the parent scale by going down a perfect 4th from C. The answer, of course, is G major. Table 8.2 will help the student remember how to find the parent scale for each type of mode.

Table 8.2 Parent Scales

Chord Type	Mode Name	Mode Number	Method of Finding the Mode
Major 7	Ionian	1	Same note
Minor 7	Dorian	2	Down a major 2nd
Minor 7, ♭2/1	Phrygian	3	Down a major 3rd
Major 7	Lydian	4	Down a perfect 4th
Dominant 7	Mixolydian	5	Down a perfect 5th
Minor 7	Aeolian	6	Down a minor 3rd
Half-diminished	Locrian	7	Up a minor 2nd

Please be aware that in everyday use, the terms *mode* and *scale* tend to be interchangeable, and one must not confuse the *D Dorian scale* with *Dorian in the key of D*. The *D Dorian scale* (or *mode*) is Dorian in the key of C, while *Dorian in the key of D* is E Dorian, the mode built on the second degree of the D major scale. In other words, when asked to sing a D Dorian scale, you sing the Dorian mode starting on the pitch D. Example 8.4 illustrates the modes and parent scales on the staff:

Example 8.4 Modes and Parent Scales

Written Assignment 8.1:

Using Modes in Composition

When using modes, it is essential that the composer use the defining characteristics of the mode effectively. Prominently feature certain notes of the mode in the melody. For instance, the scale degree that differentiates the Dorian mode from the Aeolian is the ♮6. Similarly, the ♭7 differentiates Mixolydian from Ionian, and the #4 contrasts Lydian with Ionian. The chord qualities most often define the use of Locrian and Phrygian in a composition. Mixolydian and Aeolian modes are the basis of many pop songs. Lydian and Dorian modes are the basis of many jazz compositions with Phrygian used extensively in modal jazz. You do not need to base a composition exclusively on one mode. Combine them or use them interchangeably in different ways.

Of course, even you do not use the defining characteristics of the mode in the melody; you can use them in a bass line or chord progression. Example 8.5 illustrates a slash chord progression in which the upper structures and the bass line consist of different modes:

Example 8.5 Upper Structure Progression with Two Opposing Modes

Example 8.6 demonstrates a chord progression that uses two different modes. The roots of the chords in the right hand form a descending C Phrygian mode, and the bass line consists of an ascending C Aeolian mode. The transposition of the final C of the bass line down an octave is to avoid collision with the right hand. This progression sounds a bit exotic, but it works.

More typical, however, is a song in which each section or phrase is in a different mode, or the same type of mode transposed to different pitch levels. Use of more than one mode in a melody is also quite common. Melodies often switch freely between modes. A melody may simply move between the related modes of one key with the chord progression. For instance, it could be in Dorian on the 2m chord, then Mixolydian on the 5^7 chord. Arguably, such a technique is not truly modal, because the melody is functioning within the context of a major key.

It is typical, however, in a song with slow harmonic rhythm (such as one chord to every two measures) and many of the same type of chord to use the same mode built on different pitches. For instance, consider a blues composition in the key of C, made up entirely of dominant 7th chords. The melody may be in C Mixolydian whenever the C7, or 1 chord, occurs. Similarly, on the 4 chord (F7,) the melody may be in F Mixolydian, followed by G Mixolydian on the 5 chord (G7.)

A third method is to alternate between two different modes based on the same pitch. It is common to hear a song that alternates between C Mixolydian and C Ionian, or between G Dorian and G Aeolian. Often the melody suggests one of the modes and the chord progressions suggests the other mode at different times throughout the song.

Modal Chord Progressions

A lack of a traditional cadence is a characterization of modal music. If a composition is truly modal, it will not have any authentic cadences. Model music does not use the 4-5^7-1 and 2m-5^7-1 progressions; this is what defines it as modal. Modal songs have cadences, but they are not always typical root movements of 4^{th}s and 5^{th}s.

A common Mixolydian "cadence" is the 4-♭7-1. Even though this is not an authentic cadence, the listener accepts it as a strong ending cadence.

Of course, if a composition is alternating between Ionian and some other mode, the authentic cadences may be difficult to avoid. This is acceptable, for there is no rule that says that a composer cannot mix tonality and modality.

It is also important to understand the difference between the tonal minor key and Aeolian/Dorian. Traditionally, minor in the tonal sense has one defining characteristic: use of the borrowed 5^7 chord. If a melody and chord progression is truly in Aeolian or Dorian, the 5 chord is minor. In the Dorian mode, the dominant 7th chord is the 4 chord. Similarly, in Aeolian, the dominant 7th chord is the ♭7 chord. Minor in the tonal sense usually involves the Harmonic Minor or Melodic Minor scale.

Table 8.3 lists the chords found in each mode, using Nashville numbers. 7th and important extensions are included for each chord, and Ionian is included for the sake of comparison.

Table 8.3 Modal Chords

Mode	1 chord	2 chord	3 chord	4 chord	5 chord	6 chord	7 chord
Ionian	$1\triangle^7$	$2m^7$	$3m^7$	$4\triangle^7\sharp11$	5^7	$6m^7\flat13$	$7\varnothing^7$
Dorian	$1m^7$	$2m^7$	$\flat3\triangle\sharp11$	4^7	$5m^7\flat13$	$6\varnothing$	$\flat7\triangle$
Phrygian	$\flat2/1$ (or $1m^7$)	$\flat2\triangle^7\sharp11$	$\flat3^7$	$4m^7\flat13$	$5\varnothing^7$	$\flat6\triangle^7$	$\flat7m^7$
Lydian	$1\triangle^7\sharp11$	2^7	$3m^7\flat13$	$\sharp4\varnothing^7$	$5\triangle^7$	$6m^7$	$7m^7$
Mixolydian	1^7	$2m^7\flat13$	$3\varnothing^7$	$4\triangle^7$	$5m^7$	$6m^7$	$\flat7\triangle^7\sharp11$
Aeolian	$1m^7\flat13$	$2\varnothing^7$	$\flat3\triangle^7$	$4m^7$	$5m^7$	$\flat6\triangle^7\sharp11$	$\flat7^7$
Locrian	$1\varnothing^7$	$\flat2\triangle^7$	$\flat3m^7$	$4m^7$	$\flat5\triangle^7\sharp11$	$\flat6^7$	$\flat7m^7\flat13$

Use of 7th and extensions is not required in a modal composition. A triadic chord progression will sound modal as long as the correct chord qualities are present. Table 8.4 lists some typical chord progressions for each mode. Locrian is not included in this list. Use Locrian as a chord scale for the half-diminished chord, but realize that very few (if any) pop songs have not featured Locrian.

Table 8.4 Some Typical Modal Chord Progressions

Dorian:	Phrygian:	Lydian:	Mixolydian:	Aeolian:
1m-♭7-4	♭2/1-♭3-♭6	1-2-3m-2	1-♭7-4-♭7	1m-5m-4m-5m
1m-♭3-♭7	♭2/1-♭3/1	1-2-7m-1	1-2m-♭7-1	1m-♭7-♭6-5m
1m-♭3-♭4-5m	♭2/1-♭7m-♭6	1-6m-7m-3m	1-5m-4-5m	1m-♭3-4m-♭6-5m

Using Chord Scales

More informed chord choices are possible when contemplating the use of 6th, 7th, and extended chords. Now that you have learned some of the chord scales for 7th and extended chords, it should be simple to analyze a melodic line and ascertain the proper chord scale. This may be especially helpful with a melodic passage consisting mostly of whole steps and half steps. If the line does not seem to fit the chosen mode or key, you may be able to borrow a chord from another mode. The key is to find the mode that most closely fits the line, even if it means using a 7th or extended chord.

Examples of Popular Songs Using Modes:

e *Someone Saved My Life Tonight*, by Elton John – The intro is in Ionian, but much of the verse is in Mixolydian

e *Keep On Loving You*, by REO Speedwagon – Lydian

e *Tomorrow Never Knows*, by the Beatles – Mixolydian

e *Tempted*, by Squeeze – The intro, transitions, and the first half of the chorus are in Mixolydian, and the verses alternate between Ionian and Aeolian, with several chromatic alterations thrown in

e *Karma Police*, by Radiohead – Verse alternates between Dorian and Aeolian in the chord progression, although the melody stays away from the 6th scale degree.

e *Paranoid Android*, by Radiohead – In the beginning section, the melody is in Dorian. The chord progression in that section alternates between two Dorian modes a perfect 4th apart.

e *Carry On Wayward Son*, by Kansas – Verse and chorus are in Aeolian, Instrumental interlude is in Dorian

e *Love Is Like Oxygen*, by Sweet – Aeolian

110

Written Assignment 8.2: Compose a melody of at least 16 measures using one or more modes. Harmonize the melody.

Project 2: Write a pop song that includes a verse, chorus, bridge, and possibly a pre-chorus, as well as an intro, transitions, and a coda. Include some of the harmonic and melodic elements discussed in this chapter, as well as earlier chapters. Use at least one mode besides Ionian in your melody. Present this song in lead sheet format.

Checklist of Assignments for Chapter 8

✓ **Ear-Training 8.1:** Demonstrate ability to sing/play and identify all of the modes of major, in all keys from Example 8.1.

✓ **Written Assignment 8.1:** Write out all the modes of E♭ major and B major, with corresponding chord symbols below, indicate the key signatures and provide the appropriate accidentals as well. Indicate the tetrachords contained in each mode.

✓ **Written Assignment 8.2:** Compose a melody of at least 16 measures using one or more modes. Harmonize the melody.

✓ **Project 2.0:** Write a pop song that includes a verse, chorus, bridge, and possibly a pre-chorus, as well as an intro, transitions, and a coda. Include some of the harmonic and melodic elements discussed in this chapter, as well as earlier chapters. Use at least one mode besides Ionian in your melody. Present this song in lead sheet format.

9

ADVANCED CHORD SUBSTITUTIONS

The Tritone

The Tritone, augmented 4th or diminished 5th, once thought of as "The Devil's Interval" even as recently as the Baroque period, is a very important ingredient of pop and jazz harmony. One reason is its importance in the dominant 7th chord. The ♯3 and ♭7 of a dominant 7th chord are a tritone apart. Why is this significant? Because it allows the use of *Tritone Substitutions*.

Tritone Substitutions

A tritone substitution is a specific type of chord substitution. However, before we understand *what it is*, a little background on *why it exists* is in order. There are 12 different notes in the chromatic scale, contained in one octave. Thus, it follows that there are 12 of each interval before they repeat themselves. We can test this theorem in Table 9.1, using the interval of a major 2nd.

Table 9.1 Major 2nds, Beginning on C

	First Note	Second Note
1	C	D
2	C♯ (D♭)	D♯ (E♭)
3	D	E
4	D♯ (E♭)	E♯ (F)
5	E (F♭)	F♯ (G♭)
6	F	G
7	F♯ (G♭)	G♯ (A♭)
8	G	A
9	G♯ (A♭)	A♯ (B♭)
10	A	B
11	A♯ (B♭)	B♯ (C)
12	B (C♭)	C♯ (D♭)
13	C	D

112

Note that interval number thirteen contains the same notes as interval number one. This concept is perhaps more easily understood when depicted on the musical staff, as illustrated in Example 10.1.

Example 9.1 The Number of Major 2nds within an Octave

One interval proves the exception to this rule, and that is the tritone. The reason for this exception is that the tritone dissects the octave exactly in the middle. The tritone, unlike any other interval besides the octave, is still a tritone when *inverted*. An inverted interval transposes the bottom note of the interval up an octave or the top note down an octave. Example 9.2 illustrates several intervals and their inversions, and Table 9.2 lists the inversions of all intervals smaller than an octave.

Example 9.2 Selected Intervals and Their Inversions

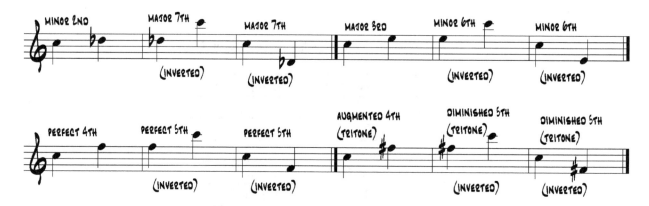

113

Table 9.2 Table of Interval Inversions within the Octave

Primary Interval	Inversion
minor 2nd	major 7th
major 2nd	minor 7th
minor 3rd	major 6th
major 3rd	minor 6th
perfect 4th	perfect 5th
augmented 4th (tritone)	diminished 5th (tritone)
diminished 5th (tritone)	augmented 4th (tritone)
perfect 5th	perfect 4th
minor 6th	major 3rd
major 6th	minor 3rd
minor 7th	major 2nd
major 7th	minor 2nd

In case the reader has been sitting on pins and needles wondering how many tritones there are in an octave, the answer is six, as shown in Example 9.3. Note that the tritones are in both augmented 4th and diminished 5th spelling.

Example 9.3 The Number of Tritones in an Octave

As stated earlier, the interval between the 3rd and 7th of a dominant seventh chord is a tritone. Since there are 12 notes in the chromatic scale, there are dominant 7th chords built on 12 different roots. If each of these dominant 7th chords contains a tritone between the 3rd and 7th, and there are only 6 tritones, then it follows that each dominant 7th chord must share these two notes (the 3rd and 7th) with another dominant 7th chord. In other words, if one were to

114

play the 3-note voicing for a dominant 7th chord, where the right hand plays the 3rd and 7th, there is one other chord in which these two notes are also the 3rd and 7th. It also happens that the roots of these two chords are a tritone apart. Furthermore, the 3rd in one chord is the 7th in the other. Example 9.4 illustrates the 6 different tritones and the dominant 7th chords that share them.

Example 9.4 Tritones and Dominant 7th Chords

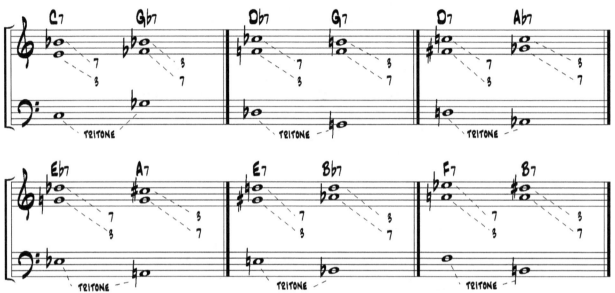

Note that the difference between these two chords is that the notes of the tritone may have a different *enharmonic spelling*. In other words, the composer would write the note differently on the staff, depending on what function it serves in the chord. For instance, C♯ and D♭ are both the same note with two different enharmonic spellings.

The term *Tritone Substitution*, also called *Tritone Sub*, refers to the use of a dominant 7th chord a tritone away in place of the original dominant 7th chord. You can produce a variety of interesting effects with this technique. Example 9.5 illustrates a short chord progression made up of dominant 7th chords:

Example 9.5 A Standard Chord Progression

C7   F7   B♭7   E♭7   A♭7

Example 9.6 illustrates the same progression, with the 2nd and 4th chords replaced with tritone substitutions:

115

Example 9.6 A Standard Chord Progression with Tri-tone Subs

Thus, this progression transforms into a descending chromatic chord progression. Note the correct enharmonic spellings of the chord tones in parentheses. Jazz frequently uses tri-tone subs. For easy reference, Table 9.3 lists the tritone sub of each dominant 7th chord:

Table 9.3 Tritone Substitutions

Primary Chord	Tritone Substitution
C7	F♯7/G♭7
C♯7/D♭7	G7
D7	G♯7/A♭7
D♯7/E♭7	A7
E7	A♯7/B♭7
F7	B7
F♯7/G♭7	C7
G7	C♯7/D♭7
G♯7/A♭7	D7
A7	D♯7/E♭7
A♯7/B♭7	E7
B7	F7

Written Assignment 9.1: Reharmonize the song in the workbook, filling in the blanks with tritone substitutions. Play through the example with the original chords, then with the tritone subs, noting the sounds and root movements.

Use of Reharmonization in Arranging and Composition

Reharmonization is an excellent tool for composers and arrangers. Arrangers will often use reharmonization to make their arrangement of a song sound unique. The difficulty in doing this is to avoid changing the melody. Therefore, the reharmonization (or *reharm*) should still fit the melody.

Of course, depending on the style of the arrangement, there can be many options to get an arranger out of a sticky situation. When appropriate, the melody can be a 6th, 7th, or extension of a chord. At times, an altered extension might even be necessary to fit the melody.

Reharms need not consist solely of tritone subs. Substitute almost any chord in place of another, as long as the cadential movement makes sense. In other words, the chord must progress from the preceding chord and into the chord following it in a way that sounds appropriate. All of the melodic harmonization techniques discussed earlier will help in such a situation.

> **Written Assignment 9.2:** Write an arrangement of a song using chord substitutions.

Many composers will take a pre-existing song, reharmonize it in such a way that it is barely recognizable, and then compose a new melody to it. This is an excellent way to "jump start" the creative process, especially when you are having trouble finding ideas. In this type of reharm, the original melody no longer matters, and the composer can play through different chord combinations until it sounds right. There may be times, however, when the progression will undergo further changes to suit the new melody.

The blues compositions of jazz legend Charlie Parker are an early example of reharmonization. Parker took the standard 12-bar blues chord progression and completely reharmonized it. Of course, this progression has few opportunities for tritone subs, so he took a different approach, using a series of 2-5 progressions to move between the chords. Parker used his blues reharmonization (with several alterations here and there) in a number of his compositions. The *Bird Blues is the title of his blues reharm.* (Charlie Parker's nickname was "Yardbird". He was often referred to as Charlie "Yardbird" Parker, but he was (and still is) often known as "Bird".) Below is an example of bird blues (Example 9.7)

Example 9.7 Bird Blues

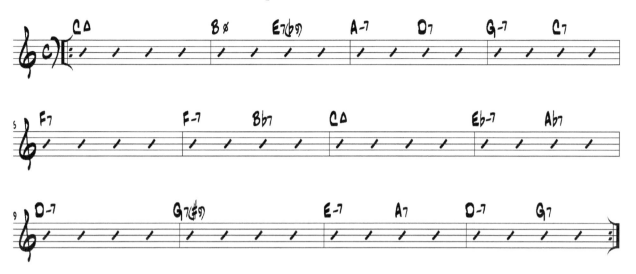

Table 9.4 illustrates a measure-by-measure comparison of the bird blues with the standard blues form.

Table 9.4 Bird Blues Compared with the Standard Blues

Measure Number	1	2	3	4	5	6	7	8		9	10	11	12
Bird Blues:	CΔ	B^{-7} $E^{7\flat9}$	A^{-7} D^7	G^{-7} C^7	F^7	F^{-7} $B\flat^7$	CΔ	$E\flat^{-7}$ $A\flat^7$	D^{-7}	$G^{7\sharp9}$	E^{-7} A^{-7}	D^{-7} G^7	
Standard Blues:	C^7	‘	‘	‘	F^7	‘	C^7	‘		G^7	F^7	C^7	‘

Note that Bird's version begins with a CΔ chord, rather than C7, and the only measures in which the two versions are the same or similar are bars 1, 5, and 7. Now look at Example 9.8:

Example 9.8 2-5 Progressions in the Bird Blues

‖ CΔ | **(2-5 in A)** B^{-7} $E^{7\flat9}$ | **(2-5 in G)** A^{-7} D^7 | **(2-5 in F)** G^{-7} C^{7+} |

| F^7 | **(2-5 in E♭)** F^{-7} $B\flat^7$ | CΔ | **(2-5 in D♭)** $E\flat^{-7}$ $A\flat^7$ |

| **(2 in C)** D^{-7} | **(5 in C)** $G^{7\sharp9}$ | **(2-5 in D)** E^{-7} A^{-7} | **(2-5 in C)** D^{-7} G^7 ‖

118

Bird's reharm of the blues consists almost entirely of 2-5 progressions. Table 10.4 above illustrates that the F7 in measure 5 is also in the standard blues. In measures 2-4, Parker uses a descending series of 2-5's to arrive at the F7 in measure 4. Measure 2 features a 2-5 in A. When the listener thinks they are in A in measure 3, it is in fact an A-7, part of the 2-5 in G. The G in measure 3 is a G-7, the $2m^7$ of a 2-5 in F.

In measure 6, the F7 becomes an F-7, the $2m^7$ of a 2-5 in E♭. Rather than move to some type of E♭ chord, the B♭7 leads to a CΔ. This is a common cadential movement in pop and jazz. We know that the most common dominant 7th chord that leads to 1 is 5^7. Furthermore, earlier in this chapter, we saw that the tritone sub for the 5^7, which can be thought of a ♭2^7, may also lead to 1. A third type of dominant 7th chord that can lead to 1 is the ♭7^7. This does not follow the traditional rules of voice leading, and this type of movement up a whole step is admittedly not as strong as a 5^7-1 or ♭2^7-1, it is still a viable option. Our ears are accustomed to hearing this progression, because it happens all the time in pop and jazz.

In measure 8, Bird uses a similar trick. Utilize a 2-5 in D♭ to progress to a 2-5 in C in measures 9 and 10. This is a variation of the tritone substitution, a 2-5 leading to another 2-5 a half step below it. Measures 9 and 10 seem to be leading us back to C. However, once we get to measures 11 and 12, we have a turnaround consisting of a 2-5 in D followed by a 2-5 in C (or a 3-6-2-5 in C.)

Many different tools are available to the composer for reharmonization. All it takes is some creativity and a good ear. By the time Charlie Parker was finished with his reharm, the only way a listener could tell it was a 12-bar blues was to count the measures!

Techniques for Reharmonization

- Tritone substitutions
- Different cadences than the original
- Non-standard cadences (such as ♭7^7-1)
- Replacing static harmony with chord movement – For instance, if the original has one chord per measure, replacing it with two or more chords per measure
- Modulations to different keys – It can be brief modulations or extended ones. A song may end up in a different key than the original due to reharmonization.
- Borrowing chords from other keys
- Using a different mode or scale – Especially effective if the song is originally in a major key.
- 6th, 7th, and extended chords – Especially useful in a new arrangement of a pre-existing song

Written Assignment 9.3: Completely reharmonize a song, and then compose a new melody for it. On your lead sheet, under the new title of the song, list the song you reharmonized in parentheses.

Checklist of Assignments for Chapter 9

✓ **Written Assignment 9.1:** Reharmonize the song below, filling in the blanks with tritone substitutions. Play through the example with the original chords, then with the tritone subs, noting the sounds and root movements

✓ **Written Assignment 9.2:** Write an arrangement of a song using chord substitutions.

✓ **Written Assignment 9.3:** Completely reharmonize a song, and then compose a new melody for it. On your lead sheet, under the new title of the song, list the song you reharmonized in parentheses.

10

CHORD-SCALE THEORY, PART 2

The Pentatonic Scale

According to many psychologists, the pentatonic scale is one of the oldest scales known to humankind, and is part of our "Collective Unconscious". According to this theory, the first songs young children sing are based on the pentatonic scale. Example 10.1 illustrates a children's nursery rhyme and melody.

Example 10.1 "It's Raining, It's Pouring"

It's rain - ing it's pour - ing, the old man is snor - ing...

The melody in Example 10.1 utilizes the 3rd, 4th and 5th degrees of the major pentatonic scale. Example 10.2 depicts the major pentatonic scale.

Example 10.2 Major Pentatonic Scale

Another form of the pentatonic scale is the minor pentatonic scale, as pictured in Example 10.3.

Example 10.3 Minor Pentatonic Scale

Note that these are the same scale, built from a different note. You can construct a series of modes from the pentatonic scale, as with any other scale. In this case, the major pentatonic is the first mode, and the minor pentatonic is the fifth mode. Example 10.4 illustrates the modes of the pentatonic scale.

Example 10.4 Modes of the Pentatonic Scale

Performers and composers alike use pentatonic scales frequently in pop music. Pentatonic patterns are also an excellent improvisational tool for playing "outside the changes", especially within the static harmony of some fusion and progressive rock. A pentatonic pattern can be played which conforms to the key, then sequenced up or down chromatically.

> **Written Assignment 10.1:** Write out all the pentatonic modes for D and G♭ pentatonic below, with accidentals.
> **Ear-Training Assignment 10.1:** Practice identifying all the modes of the pentatonic scale.

The Blues Scale

The blues scale contains six notes, not including the octave. It is built on the minor pentatonic scale with an inserted chromatic note between the 3rd and 4th degrees, as illustrated in Example 10.5.

Example 10.5 The Blues and Minor Pentatonic Scales

Popular music, especially Rock frequently uses the blues scale. Furthermore, most Rock guitar solos exclusively featured the blues scale in the 50's, 60's and 70's. The trick, of course, is to know how to use the scale. The second and fourth degrees of the scale, in this case, the E♭ and F♯, are the "blue" notes, and these can add harmonic interest to a line. Example 10.6 illustrates the relationship of these notes to the chord tones of a C7 chord, the 1 chord in the C blues.

Example 10.6 "Blue" Notes

Note the use of the ♮11. The use of this tone is not frowned upon in the context of the blues, although it is preferable not to dwell on the note too long. One could use the C blues over an entire chorus of the basic C blues.

There is yet another blues scale built on the major pentatonic scale, with an inserted chromatic note between the 2nd and 3rd degrees, as illustrated in Example 10.7. As there is no standard name for this blues scale, we will call it the *Major Blues Scale*.

Example 10.7 Major Pentatonic and Major Blues Scales

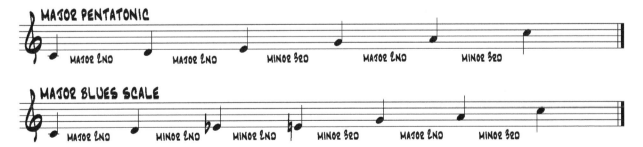

Bebop Scales

Some scales were most likely invented by accident, and then codified later by other musicians who have analyzed recordings. The *Bebop Scales* are perhaps an example of this.

Example 10.8 Bebop Scales

Note that all of these bebop scales contain some variation on the three-note chromatic line found in the blues scale. In fact, they are a normal 7-note scale with an added chromatic note. For instance, the Bebop Dominant scale is a Mixolydian mode with an added ♭7, and the Bebop Dorian is a Dorian mode with an added ♭3. The Bebop Major is a major scale with an added ♯5, and the Bebop Melodic Minor is a Melodic Minor scale (or Dorian with a ♭7) with an added ♯5. Of course, the added chromatic notes function as passing tones. Employed extensively in jazz, bebop scales are quite common in the Blues and in pop.

The Diminished Scale

The major scale contains only one tritone interval, between the 4th and 7th degrees. Earlier in these pages, we discussed the fact that the major scale is an *Asymmetric Scale*, or a scale with an odd number of notes and unequal number of intervals. A scale with an even number of notes and an equal number of intervals is a *Symmetric Scale*. Two such scales are the Diminished and Whole-Tone scales. In addition, both of these scales contain more than one tritone interval.

The diminished scale derives its name from the fact that it is two fully diminished 7th chords a whole-step apart, as illustrated in Example 10.9:

Example 10.9 Diminished Scale

Note that the scale contains four tritones. Furthermore, every note in the scale has a corresponding note a tritone away.

The diminished scale is composed of alternating whole-steps and half steps. There are eight notes in the diminished scale, and it contains four whole-steps and four half steps. Two forms of the diminished scale are used, the whole-step half-step version, which is simply known as the diminished scale, and the half-step whole-step version, also known as the *Auxiliary Diminished Scale.* Example 10.10 illustrates both forms of the scale, along with appropriate chords and chord symbols:

Example 10.10 Diminished and Auxiliary Diminished Scales

The chord which is built from the diminished scale is a fully-diminished 7th chord, in this case, C°7. Note that it would not work with a half-diminished chord, because there is no ♭7. Of more interest, however, is the variety of dominant 7th chord built from the auxiliary diminished scale. Above is a C7 with a ♭9 and ♯9, ♯11, ♭5 and ♮13. The inclusion of two different 9th degrees is necessary because this scale contains eight notes, rather than seven. When singing the scale over the appropriate chord, one should learn the auxiliary diminished from the root of the chord, as well as the diminished from the ♭9.

The Whole-Tone Scale

The Whole-Tone Scale is a six-note symmetric scale made up entirely of whole steps. There are only two whole-tone scales, as each note of the whole-tone scale is the root of another whole-tone scale made up of the same notes. Example 10.11 illustrates the C whole-tone scale, and the associated chord symbol.

Example 10.11 The Whole-Tone Scale

Note that the chord based on this scale contains a ♮9 and ♮3, ♯11 and ♯5, and ♭7.

Just as the diminished scale is made up of two fully diminished 7th chords a whole-step apart, the whole-tone scale can be thought of as two augmented triads a whole-step apart, as illustrated in Example 10.12.

Example 10.12 Whole-Tone Scale: Augmented Triads

As illustrated above, the whole-tone scale contains three tritone intervals, and once again, each note has a corresponding note a tritone away.

> **Written Assignment 10.2:** Write out the requested scales on the staves in the workbook.
> **Ear-Training Assignment 10.2:** Practice identifying the blues scales, bebop scales, diminished and auxiliary diminished scales, and the whole-tone scale.

Use of the Scales in Composition

All of the scales explained in this chapter are extremely useful for chord progressions and melodies. In particular, pentatonic, blues and bebop scales allow the composer to write music that sounds tonal without resorting to the major scale. Of course, use of the diminished and whole tones scales will introduce a degree of dissonance into a composition, but this can be useful as well.

Many of the melodies found in Black Gospel, R&B, and Hip-Hop are from either the Pentatonic or the Minor Blues scales. Roc and Blues often use the Blues and Bebop scales. Whole-Tone and Diminished scales are not as often made use of for the basis of a composition. However, isolated melodic passages can contain these scales with the proper chord, and guitarists often use both scales for solos.

> **Written Assignment 10.3:** Compose a melody of at least 16 measures using one or more of the scales in this chapter. Harmonize the melody.

Checklist of Assignments for Chapter 10

✓ **Written Assignment 10.1:** Write out all the pentatonic modes for D and G♭ pentatonic below, with accidentals.

✓ **Ear-Training Assignment 10.1:** Practice identifying all the modes of the pentatonic scale

✓ **Written Assignment 10.2:** Write out the requested scales in the examples.

✓ **Ear-Training Assignment 10.2:** Practice identifying the blues scales, bebop scales, diminished and auxiliary diminished scales, and the whole-tone scale.

✓ **Written Assignment 10.3:** Compose a melody of at least 16 measures using one or more of the scales in this chapter. Harmonize the melody.

11

CHORD-SCALE THEORY, PART 3

Melodic Minor

Example 11.1 Modes of Melodic Minor

130

In the Classical tradition, the ascending form of the Melodic Minor scale is played with a raised 6th and 7th degree, and the descending form is in "Natural Minor," or Aeolian. The melodic minor scale in jazz (and pop, for that matter) features the raised 6th and 7th whether ascending or descending. Thus, the ascending form is the *Jazz Melodic Minor*. There are several ways of looking at the melodic minor scale. One way is as a major scale with a ♭3. Another viewpoint, which we will adopt for the purposes of this lesson, is as a Dorian scale with a raised 7th. Each of the melodic minor modes has several accepted names, but in the system we will use, the base, tonic, or first mode is "Dorian ♯7", with the naming of the other modes in relation to that mode name. Example 11.1 illustrates the modes of melodic minor.

There are a number of interesting facets of this scale deserving of mention. One of the most striking of these is the unusual placement of whole steps and half steps. The melodic minor scale contains two half steps, just as the major scale does; however, the distribution and order of the whole steps and half steps is different from the major scale. In the major scale, as discussed in an earlier chapter, two whole steps separate the two half steps. In the melodic minor scale, the two half steps are separated by four whole steps (between the 3rd scale degree and the 7th scale degree) and one half step (between the root and 2nd scale degree.) In Example 11.2, the Melodic Minor scale is in two octaves, so the reader can see the distribution of whole steps and half steps:

Example 11.2 Melodic Minor Scale Distribution of Half- and Whole-steps

It is also helpful to look at the *Tetrachords* contained in the modes of melodic minor. Two tetrachords make up the 7-note asymmetric scale from the root to the octave (which actually totals eight notes, including the octave,). The term Tetrachord describes the three intervals contained in a grouping of four notes, from the Latin root Tetra, meaning three. Example 11.3 illustrates five types of tetrachords.

Example 11.3 Tetrachords

Note the diminished tetrachord in the example. The intervals are half-whole-half, like the first three notes of the auxiliary diminished scale.

131

The two tetrachords will always share a note in common. In the form we will use, the common note will be the root of the mode. Thus, each mode is composed of two tetrachords, and we must be aware of the interval between the two tetrachords. This will help the reader understand the order of half steps and whole steps in each mode. Example 11.4 illustrates the tetrachords found in the modes of melodic minor.

Example 11.4 Tetrachords Found in the Modes of Melodic Minor

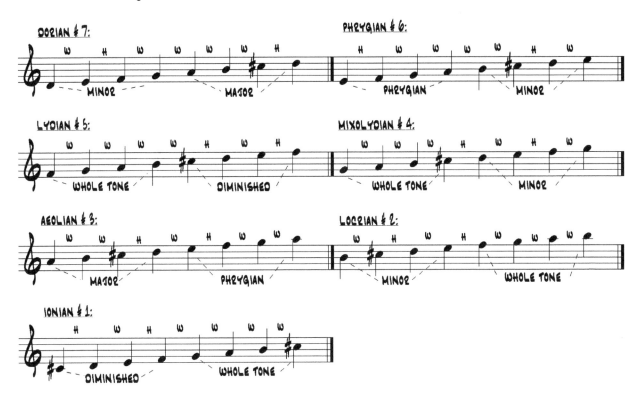

Note the diminished tetrachord followed by a whole-tone tetrachord in the 7th mode, Ionian ♯1. That is why this scale is sometimes known as the Diminished/Whole-tone Scale. For readers who find tetrachords helpful in remembering the scales and modes, Table 11.1 lists them.

Table 11.1 Tetrachords Found in the Modes of Melodic Minor

Mode Name	Tetrachord 1	Tetrachord 2	Interval Between Tetrachords
Dorian ♯7	Minor	Whole Tone	Whole Step
Phrygian ♮6	Phrygian	Major	Whole Step
Lydian ♯5	Whole Tone	Minor	Whole Step
Mixolydian ♯4	Whole Tone	Diminished	Half Step
Aeolian ♮3	Major	Minor	Whole Step
Locrian ♮2	Minor	Phrygian	Half Step
Ionian ♯1	Diminished	Whole Tone	Whole Step

Use of the Modes of Melodic Minor

Jazz and pop frequently use the modes of melodic minor especially the Lydian Dominant, Locrian ♮2 and Altered Scale (Ionian♯1). The Lydian Dominant is essentially the Mixolydian mode with a ♯4. This renders it extremely useful as a method of circumventing the dreaded ♮4 avoid tone in dominant 7th chords. The Locrian ♮2 is preferable to the Locrian mode for use with the half-diminished 7th chord, due to the ♮9. Utilize the Ionian ♯1 with the altered dominant 7th (such as G7alt,) a chord in which the composer altered all of the extensions. Due to the unique juxtaposition of half-steps and whole-steps, the fourth degree of the scale is actually the ♮3 of the chord. The second and third degrees are the ♭9 and ♯9, respectively. The altered dominant 7th chord has been used extensively in jazz since the Bebop era.

The remaining modes are very important in modal jazz, even though composers use them infrequently. The minor-major 7th chord uses the Dorian ♯7, and the augmented major 7th chord uses the Lydian ♯5.The chord symbol found in modal jazz for Phrygian ♮6 would more likely be F+/E than E-7♭9, as pictured in Example 11.1. Aeolian ♮3 is probably used the least of all of them, as most dominant 7th chords with a ♭13 would also contain some sort of altered 9th. Table 11.2 illustrates the chord symbols used for each mode, the mode name, parent scale, and simplest method of finding the parent scale from the root of the chord. C is the basis for all chord symbols.

Table 11.2 Chord Scales for Melodic Minor

Chord Symbol	Mode	Parent Minor Scale	Method of Finding Parent Scale
C-Δ7	C Dorian ♯7	C Melodic	Root of mode
D♭+/C, C-13♭9	C Phrygian ♮6	B♭ Melodic	Down major 2nd
CΔ7+5	C Lydian Augmented	A Melodic	Down minor 3rd
C13♯11	C Mixolydian ♯4	G Melodic	Down perfect 4th
C9♭13	C Aeolian ♮3	F Melodic	Up perfect 4th
CØ7	C Locrian ♮2	E♭ Melodic	Up minor 3rd
C7alt.	C Ionian ♯1	D♭ Melodic	Up minor 2nd

Augmented-Major 7 Upper-structures

Example 11.5 Augmented-Major 7 Upper-Structures

For keyboard, melody, and improvisation purposes, there is an augmented-major 7 upper-structure chord that is very useful with all of the modes of melodic minor. The chord is built off the ♭3 of the parent melodic minor scale. Example 11.5 illustrates the chord tone in each chord that serves as the root of the augmented-major 7 upper-structure. This information is very important in learning how to use these upper-structures.

> **Ear-Training Assignment 11.1:** Learn to sing and identify the augmented-major 7 upper-structure voicing pictured in Example 11.5 for the Mixolydian #4, Locrian ♮2 and Ionian #1 modes, in all keys.

Minor 2-5-1

Example 11.6 illustrates two piano voicings for the minor 2-5-1 progression with extensions. Note that the 2 is a half-diminished chord, and the 5 is an altered dominant chord.

Example 11.6 Minor 2-5-1

In jazz harmony, a minor 2-5 is often "borrowed", leading to a major 7th or dominant 7th chord, as illustrated in Example 11.7. We will call this an "Altered" 2-5-1.

Example 11.7 Altered 2-5-1

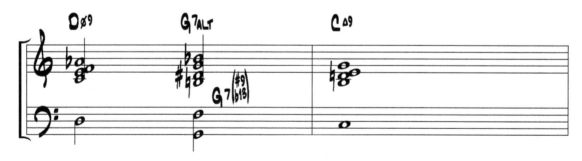

> **Keyboard Assignment 11.1:** Demonstrate ability to play the voicings for the minor and altered 2-5-1's pictured in Example 11.6 and Example 11.7, in all keys.

Harmonic Minor

The Harmonic Minor scale is perhaps more difficult to learn than melodic minor, partly due to the augmented 2nd interval between the 6th and 7th degrees.

Example 11.8 The Modes of Harmonic Minor

Example 11.8 illustrates the modes of harmonic minor, and associated chords. The mode most frequently used in jazz and pop is the Phrygian #3, which is sometimes also called the "Eastern Scale" due to the augmented 2nd between the 2nd and 3rd degrees.

Advanced Upper-Structures

Chapter 4 addressed the issue of upper-structure triads, consisting only of the extensions of the chord. From this point on, we will deal mostly with upper-structure 7th chords. Augmented-Major 7 upper-structure 7th chords from the melodic minor scale have already been discussed, and these are extremely useful. There are also a number of other upper-structure chords. It is perhaps easiest at first to think of them as slash chords, with the upper-structure as the top chord and the root, third and fifth or seventh as the bottom chord, which we will call the "base" chord. Table 11.3 illustrates this method, using C as the root for each chord.

Table 11.3 Advanced Upper-Structures

Chord	Base Chord	Upper-Structure	Slash Chord	Extensions	Scale/Mode
CΔ13♯11	C triad	B-7	$\frac{\text{B-7}}{\text{C}}$	♮9 ♯11 ♭13	Lydian
C-13	C- triad	B♭Δ	$\frac{\text{B♭Δ}}{\text{C-}}$	♮9 ♮11 ♭13	Dorian
C13♯11	C triad	B♭Δ♯5	$\frac{\text{B♭Δ♯5}}{\text{C}}$	♮9 ♯11 ♭13	Mixolydian ♯4 (Mel. min.)
C9+5(♯11)	C+ triad	B♭+ triad	$\frac{\text{B♭+}}{\text{C+}}$	♯5 ♮9 ♯11	Whole-tone
C13♭9♯9	C root or C7	B♭°7 or E♭°7	B♭°7/C or $\frac{\text{E♭°7}}{\text{C7}}$	♭9 ♯9 ♯11 ♭13	Auxiliary Diminished
C7 alt.	C7(no5)	EΔ♯5	$\frac{\text{EMaj7♯5}}{\text{C7(no5)}}$ or B♭ø7/C	♭9 ♯9 ♯11 ♭13	Ionian♯1 (Mel. min.)
Cø7	C° triad	G♭Δ♯5 or B♭7	$\frac{\text{G♭Δ♯5}}{\text{C°}}$ or $\frac{\text{B♭7}}{\text{C°}}$	♭5 ♮9 ♮11 ♭13	Locrian ♮2 (Mel. min.)

As illustrated in Table 11.3, a major $13^{th}\sharp 11$ chord consists of a major triad on the bottom and a minor 7th chord from the $\flat 7$ on top. A minor 13th chord is comprised of a minor triad on the bottom, and a major 7th chord beginning on the $\flat 7$ on top. For the dominant 13th chord, we will use the Lydian Dominant form, because the $\sharp 11$ is usually preferable to the $\natural 11$ avoid tone. Thus, the upper-structure chord consists of an augmented major 7th chord from the $\flat 7$, and the base chord is a major triad. The dominant 9th chord with an augmented 5th is derived from the Whole-Tone Scale. The slash chord consists of an augmented triad on the bottom, and an augmented triad from the $\flat 7$ on top. The dominant 7th chord with a $\flat 9$, $\sharp 9$, $\sharp 11$, $\natural 13$ and $\natural 5$ is derived from the Diminished Scale. This has two possible fully-diminished 7th chord upper-structures, one from the $\flat 7$ and one from the $\sharp 9$. Note that the first slash chord contains a 7th chord upper-structure over the root, rather than over a base triad. Example 11.9 illustrates the $\natural 3$ in the upper-structure. The composer may utilize two possible upper-structure chords with the altered dominant 7th chord. The first is the augmented-major 7th chord built from the $\sharp 3$, as discussed earlier in this chapter, which contains a $\sharp 9$. The second upper-structure is a half-diminished 7th chord built from the $\flat 7$, and contains the $\flat 9$ as well as the $\natural 3$. Similarly, two upper-structure 7th chords are available for a half-diminished 7th chord. In addition to the augmented-major 7th chord built from the $\flat 5$, a dominant 7th chord built from the $\flat 7$ is useful.

Example 11.9 Advanced Upper-Structures

The upper-structure 7th chord for the fully diminished 7th chord was briefly discussed in earlier in the chapter. It consists of a fully diminished chord a whole-step above the root, as illustrated in Example 11.10.

Example 11.10 Upper-Structure 7th Chord for the Diminished 7th Chord

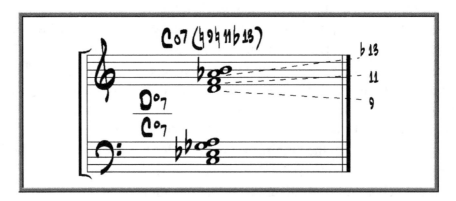

Synthetic Scales

Musicians have concocted a number of additional scales over the years for use in improvisation and composition. These scales are *Synthetic Scales*. This movement was perhaps inspired in part by the work of the late musicologist Nicolas Slonimsky, whose "Thesaurus of Scales and Melodic Patterns" (Slonimsky 1947) has been widely studied by musicians such as John Coltrane. The Blues Scale and the Bebop Scales can also be thought of as synthetic scales, although they were probably not devised in the mathematical manner that some modern synthetic scales are.

Augmented and Tritone Scales

Combining the notes of two triads into a scale can form other types of synthetic scales. Example 11.11 illustrates two such scales, the *Augmented Scale* and the *Tritone Scale*.

Example 11.11 Augmented and Tritone Scales

The Augmented scale consists of two augmented triads a half-step apart, and the tritone scale is constructed from two major triads a tritone apart. A C13♯5♭9 chord could utilize an augmented scale, even though the ♭7 is not actually in the scale. Taking into consideration the fact that an augmented 2nd and a minor 3rd are different enharmonic spellings for the same interval, the tritone scale can be called a symmetric scale, in that it has an even number of notes, and contains two half-steps, two whole-steps and two minor thirds.

Constructing Synthetic Scales

The possibilities for inventing synthetic scales are practically endless. Construct them using any raw materials, including triads, 7th chords, a sequence of intervals, or tetrachords. For instance, Example 11.13 illustrates a synthetic scale formed by combining a C blues scale tetrachord (Example 11.12) and a G blues scale tetrachord, which we will call the "Bebop Blues Scale".

Example 11.12 Blues Scale Tetrachord

Example 11.13 "Bebop Blues Scale"

A synthetic scale can even span two octaves with no repeated notes. Of course, such a scale would most likely contain all 12 tones of the chromatic scale. Slonimsky's (1986) "Complementary Scales" is a good example.

Written Assignment 11.1: Identify the modes and parent melodic minor scales for the following chords.
Written Assignment 11.2: Devise a synthetic scale, and indicate the type of chord to use with it.

Chord-Scale Theory Revisited

In an earlier chapter, we dealt with the common modes of the major scale used in pop and jazz. At this point, however, the student has a considerably larger number of available chord-scale options. Table 11.4 lists the scales for use with 7th and extended chords.

Table 11.4 Most Common Scales/Modes Used with Standard Jazz Chords, Part 2

Chord Symbol	Scales/Modes Used
CΔ, CΔ9, C6	Ionian, Lydian, Bebop Major, Major Pentatonic, Major Blues
CΔ7♯11, CΔ9♯11	Lydian
CΔ7♯5, CΔ9♯5	Lydian♯5 (Mel.), Ionian♯5 (Harm.), Bebop Major
C-7, C-9, C-11	Dorian, Minor Pentatonic, Minor Blues (Blues Scale), Bebop Dorian
C-Δ	Dorian♯7 (Mel.), Bebop Melodic Minor, Aeolian♯7
C7, C9, C13	Mixolydian♯4 (Mel.), Mixolydian, Minor Pentatonic, Major Pentatonic, Minor Blues, Major Blues, Bebop Dominant, Bebop Dorian
C7♯5	Whole-Tone, Ionian♯1 (Mel.), Augmented Scale
C9♯5	Whole-Tone
C7♭9	Auxiliary Diminished, Ionian♯1*, Phrygian♮3 (Harm.), Tritone Scale, Augmented Scale*
C13♭9	Auxiliary Diminished, Tritone Scale, Augmented Scale
C7♯9	Auxiliary Diminished, Ionian♯1*, Minor Pentatonic, Minor Blues, Major Blues, Bebop Dorian
C13♯9	Auxiliary Diminished, Minor Pentatonic, Minor Blues, Major Blues, Bebop Dorian
C7♯11	Mixolydian♯4, Minor Blues, Whole-Tone*, Tritone Scale*
C9♯11, C13♯11	Mixolydian♯4, Minor Blues
C7♭13	Aeolian♮3 (Mel.), Phrygian♮3 (Harm.), Ionian♯1*
C9♭13	Aeolian♮3
C7alt.	Ionian♯1
C°7	Diminished
Cø7	Locrian♮2 (Mel.), Locrian, Locrian ♮6 (Harm.)
Cø9	Locrian♮2
D♭/C	Phrygian
D♭+/C	Phrygian♮6

*More useful if piano is not playing the ♮5
(Mel.=Melodic Minor, Harm.=Harmonic Minor)

Use of Scales in Composition

Of the modes of Melodic and Harmonic Minor, Phrygian ♮6, Mixolydian ♯4 (Melodic Minor) and Phrygian ♮3 (Harmonic Minor) are probably used most as the basis for a composition. However, Ionian ♯1 and Locrian ♮2 are used quite often in association with the altered dominant 7th and the half-diminished chord, respectively. The Tritone Scale sounds even more "Eastern" than the Phrygian ♮3, and it is very useful if the goal is a more exotic sound.

Use most of these scales exclusively for a composition, or for isolated melodic passages.

> **Written Assignment 11.3:** Compose a melody of at least 16 measures using one or more of the modes listed in this chapter, or the synthetic scale you devised. Harmonize the melody.

Checklist of Assignments for Chapter 11

- ✓ **Ear-Training Assignment 11.1:** Learn to sing and identify the augmented-major 7 upper-structure voicing pictured in Example 11.5 for the Mixolydian ♯4, Locrian ♮2 and Ionian ♯1 modes, in all keys.
- ✓ **Keyboard Assignment 11.1:** Demonstrate ability to play the voicings for the minor and altered 2-5-1's pictured in Example 11.6 and Example 11.7, in all keys.
- ✓ **Written Assignment 11.1:** Identify the modes and parent melodic minor scales for the following chords
- ✓ **Written Assignment 11.2:** Devise a synthetic scale, and indicate the type of chord needed to support it.
- ✓ **Written Assignment 11.3:** Compose a melody of at least 16 measures using one or more of the scales or modes listed in this chapter, or the synthetic scale you devised. Harmonize the melody.

12

ARRANGING FOR RHYTHM SECTION AND VOCALS

In the early days of pop music, composers often worked for publishing houses that employed staff arrangers and copyists. In fact, it was not uncommon for a composer to write only the melody, lyrics, and let the staff arrangers set the melody to a chord progression. Modern composers, especially those on a budget, compose the lyrics, melody, and chord changes, arrange the music and produce the demo recording.

Most composers will find occasions when a simple lead sheet or chord chart is not adequate, and must write a separate part for each instrument. A majority of the time, each part will consist of a chord chart combined with the notation of specific riffs. In fact, the notation techniques used for lead sheets are nearly identical to those used for instrumental parts. This chapter will focus on the "rhythm section", which is the standard configuration of drums, bass, guitar and keyboards found in most of today's popular music, as well as backing vocals.

Common Techniques for Instrumental Parts

Instrumental parts (also known as "charts") will rarely, if ever, include the melody. The most important objective is to keep the number of pages to a minimum. While keyboardists can often take time to turn pages in the course of a song, drummers, bassists and guitarists usually cannot. Consequently, it is important that each part be no more than three or four pages long. Instrumentalists can spread a four-page chart across two music stands with no need to turn pages.

It is helpful if the charts follow the same format as the lead sheet. Thus, the composer can use the lead sheet as a guide during rehearsal. It is imperative that all the charts follow a uniform format if the lead sheet varies from the instrumental charts. In other words, measure numbers or section letters must match, and each section of the song must be in the same place in each chart. Here is an example: A song contains an eight-measure repeated section. Originally, the composer intended to score the eight measures with a repeat sign on each end. However, the synth player plays a certain riff the first time through, followed by a completely different riff when they repeat the section. There are several ways to handle such a dilemma. The first method is to break the synth part into two staves at this point. The top staff will be labeled "1st time only" and contain the first riff to be played. The bottom staff will then contain the 2nd riff, and it will state "2nd time only" (Example 12.1.)

Example 12.1 Synth Part in Two Staves

Note the use of the bracket to differentiate the set of two staves from the single-staff system above it.

This solution to the problem, while not unheard-of, could perhaps be a bit confusing to the keyboardist. Rather, the best solution is to eliminate the repeat sign and score the repeat as eight additional measures. The same alteration must also occur in all the other instrumental parts.

Planning Ahead

It is always a good idea to plan by mapping out each section of the song on paper before writing out the parts. In classical and big band compositions, the composer will usually write a score containing each part on a separate staff or set of staves, then copy each part separately from the score. Modern computer music notation programs, such as Finale and Sibelius, allow the user to "extract" each part of a score to a separate file. It is not typically necessary to notate modern pop arrangements in a score format, but there may be times when it proves useful. Of course, a composition that includes acoustic horns and strings requires a conductor and a score.

Format

Write charts on 8 1/2 by 11 paper or oversize score paper for big band or orchestra. In most situations, the 8 1/2 by 11 format is adequate. The top of the first page should contain the title, centered an often underlined, followed by the name of the composer(s) and the name of arranger, if applicable. The first system of page one is usually placed approximately two inches down from the top of the page. On the following pages, place the first system one inch from the top.

Indicate the groove, musical style, and/or tempo above the first measure. It is usually underlined or bordered by a rectangle with rounded edges (Figure 12.1.)

145

Figure 12.1 Groove Indication

If the musical style, groove or tempo changes in the course of the song, indicate it in the same way, above the system at the beginning of the measure in which it first occurs. If the groove or tempo changes in the middle of a measure (which is very rare,) place it above the beat in which it occurs.

The top left-hand corner of the first page of the chart should contain the name of the instrument. This text can be almost as large as the title, and you may choose to underline it. Indicate the instrument name in smaller type on the top of each of the following pages, in either the left or the right corner.

The preferred technique for page numbering is to indicate the name of the song (it can be abbreviated if needed,) followed by a hyphen (-) and the page number. Underline and center this text just above the top system of the page, high enough to avoid clashing with chord symbols.

As discussed in chapter three, major section numbers or letters should be placed at the beginning of a system whenever possible, and placed within a circle or box. Place a double bar at the end of each section. When using letters to label the sections of a chart or lead sheet, it is important to remember the performers will use these for rehearsal and performance. Label each major section sequentially, regardless of the form of the song. In other words, a song with an A-A-B-A-B-C-B form will read A-B-C-D-E-F-G in the chart.

Follow every item in the Lead Sheet Checklist at the end of chapter three when writing charts (a new checklist which includes all of those items is provided at the end of this chapter as well.)

Common Notation Issues

Most rhythm section charts will consist largely of slashes with chords above them (with the exception of drum charts, which usually only contain slashes.) Notate chord changes following syncopated rhythms using slash or diamond note heads, as discussed in chapter three.

Tempo and Groove/Musical Style Indications

In classical music, tempo markings consist of words such as Allegro and Andante. In modern pop music, especially since the advent of sampling, precision is extremely important. Indicate tempos by the number of beats per minute (bpm) as illustrated in Figure 12.2:

$$\boxed{q = 120}$$

Figure 12.2 Tempo Indication

Groove has never been a consideration in classical music. Pop music, however, is rooted in rhythm, and groove is one of the most important components. Furthermore, most of the terms used to describe the groove also describe the musical style. Some of the most common terms used to indicate groove and/or musical style are:

Bluegrass	Funk Shuffle	Pop	Rock Ballad
Blues Shuffle	Gospel	Pop Ballad	Rock Shuffle
Bossa Nova	Gospel Rock	Punk	Rockabilly
Country	Hard Rock	R&B	Samba
Country Swing	Heavy Metal	R&B Ballad	Shuffle
Disco	Hip-Hop Shuffle	Reggae	Ska
Funk	New Wave	Rock	Swing

Often a combination of the groove/style indication and the bpm is required. Typically, you should list the groove/style above the bpm, and the bpm will be in parentheses. There are really no set rules regarding groove and style indications. It is more important that the marking clearly indicates the desired groove and style. Often, the words "slow", "medium" and "fast" will assist in making the meaning clear, such as "Slow Funk". At times, a composer may have patterned his/her song on the drum beat of another popular song or group, and the title or group name is in the groove indication, such as "'Walk This Way' Groove". Terms from dance and techno, such as "Drum and Bass" or "trance" are also used. Of course, if some of the musicians in the band know nothing about dance music, these terms will not be very helpful. There is a good chance that the composer will occasionally need to demonstrate a groove by playing a similar recording anyway, but it is still a good idea to make groove markings as descriptive as possible.

Multi-measure Rests

Use a "multi-measure rest" for groups of adjacent full-measure rests with a combined duration longer than two measures. The symbol for a multi-measure rest is a long horizontal line with a vertical line on each end, with the number of measures centered directly above the horizontal line. The multi-measure rest in Figure 12.2 indicates six measures of rests.

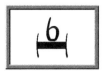

Figure 12.3 Multi-Measure Rest

A multi-measure rest can lie within the space of a single measure, or across an entire system. There is usually a bar line on either side of the symbol. When using multi-measure rests, it is important that the beginning of each new section is easily recognizable. For instance, you must separate eight measures of rest beginning with the fifth bar of section B and ending in the fifth bar of section C into two groupings of four-measure rests, as illustrated in Example 12.2:

Example 12.2 Multi-Measure Rests Between Sections

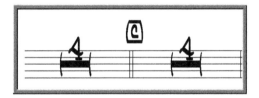

Multi-measure rests can only contain full-measure rests. Display a full measure even if only a few beats of a measure contain rests.

Fills

Occasionally, a composer may feel that several beats at the end of a phrase require a short improvised line from the drums, guitar, bass or keyboard, or a "fill". Fills are quite common in the blues and in pop music as well. The duration of a fill can be anywhere from one beat to several measures. Indicate the length of a fill by the word "fill" followed by a horizontal line. At the end of the horizontal line, a very short vertical line stretches down toward the staff to indicate the end of the fill (Example 12.3.)

Example 12.3 Fill Marking

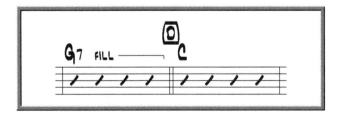

Place the word "fill" directly above the beat in which it begins. If it is to begin on a subdivision of a beat, indicate it in the notation on the staff (Example 12.4.)

148

Example 12.4 Fill Beginning on a Rhythmic Subdivision of a Beat

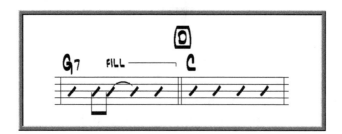

Articulations

While pop and jazz use the same articulation markings as classical, they perhaps differ slightly in practice. The Staccato (.) indicates a short, unaccented note. The Tenuto (-) indicates that the note should be held to its' full value, unaccented but at the same volume throughout the note. A "Teepee Accent", or "Teepee," (^) indicates a note played at a medium to loud dynamic level in a short and percussive style. Often the teepee is not as short as a staccato, especially in swing and shuffle styles. A note with an accent mark (>) should be played to its' full value, but with a sharp attack and decay. The Marcato (≥) indicates that a note should be held to its' full value with no diminution, with a percussive attack and a medium to loud dynamic level. Use the teepee and staccato on note values of one beat or less.

Use the Slur on a series of notes, and do not confuse it with a Tie. When a series of notes are slurred, the first note is articulated and the remaining slurred notes are played smoothly with no articulation (Example 12.5.)

Example 12.5 Slur

(Source: Lindsay, 1985)

Improvised Solos

When an instrument has an improvised solo, notate the chord changes with slashes and rhythmic notation as usual. However, place the word "solo" above the staff at the beginning of the measure in which it starts. Additionally, place the words "end solo" above the staff at the end of the measure in which it is completed. It is also a good idea to indicate in the other parts in parentheses that there is a solo "(guitar solo)" as well as where the solo ends "(end guitar solo)."

Rhythm Section Instruments

In addition to the items mentioned above, there are a few characteristic traits of the individual instruments that need explanation. There are different ways to notate each instrument. For instance, some instruments are *transposing* instruments, while some are considered *nontransposing* instruments. The piano is a nontransposing instrument, in that the notated pitch and the sounded pitch are the same. On a transposing instrument, the notated pitch is different from the played pitch. In the next section, we will explain the transpositions of the rhythm section instruments.

Keyboards

Keyboards (piano, synthesizer, organ, clav, Rhodes, etc.) are nontransposing instruments. The usable range of the piano, as well as most synthesizers, is virtually unlimited (Example 12.6.) Even a synthesizer with less than 88 keys can be transposed, if needed.

Example 12.6 Range of the Piano/Keyboard

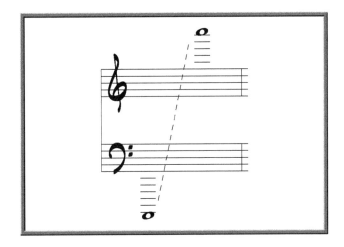

When writing for keyboard, one or two staves may be used. If two staves are used, they should be in brackets. If the keyboard part consists largely of chord symbols and slash notation, notate the part on one staff, usually in the treble clef. If the keyboardist is playing several keyboards at a time, it is wise to use two staves, even if they are both in treble clef, and label each at the beginning of the song (i.e., "synth 1" and "synth 2" or "Triton" and "K2500.") When labeling staves, it is a good idea to indent the first system on the first page.

If one synthesizer is playing chord changes and the other is playing riffs or "stabs" (percussive chords, usually played with a brass sound) the keyboardist would play the riffs in the right hand and the changes in the left hand. It is probably best to put the riffs in the top staff and the chord changes in the bottom. If in doubt, however, check with the keyboardist first. Example 12.7 illustrates the first two measures of a keyboard chart for two synthesizers:

Example 12.7 Keyboard Chart For Two Synthesizers

If one synthesizer is only used for chords and the other for melodic lines, or if the keyboardist is just using one keyboard and playing chords in the left hand and riffs in the right hand, it is also acceptable to use only one staff, placing the riffs on the staff and chord changes above it.

We have already discussed methods for writing specific rhythms for chord symbols. However, there may be occasions where a composer may desire a specific voicing as well. There are two methods for achieving this: 1.) Write out the voicings note for note, or 2.) Write out the top note of the voicing along with the chord symbol. Example 12.8 illustrates the latter method.

Example 12.8 Top Note of Piano Voicing with Chord Symbols

Note that the stems extend beyond the top of the note head. This is the preferred method for indicating that a specific voicing is required with a certain note on top. The stem should extend to the normal length below the note head, then perhaps 1/4 of the way past the top. Of course, the long part of the stem should point up on the low notes as in Example 12.9.

Example 12.9 Top Note Piano Voicing with Stems Pointing Up

Be aware that this style of notation may be easier to read with the stems pointing down, as in Example 12.8. In this case, it is acceptable to break the rules regarding stems.

There may be occasions where a composer may need a grand staff (2 staves) only during certain sections of the song. It is up to the arranger to decide if switching between a single staff and a grand staff several times throughout the song will be confusing to the keyboardist. If the grand staff is only occasionally required, this may be acceptable. It may be safer to use a grand staff throughout the entire song, leaving the bass clef staff empty when it is not in use.

Guitar

The guitar is a transposing instrument whose parts are one octave higher than it sounds. Example 12.10 illustrates the concert range of the guitar, and Example 12.11 the written range.

Example 12.10 Concert Range of the Guitar

Example 12.11 Written Range of the Guitar

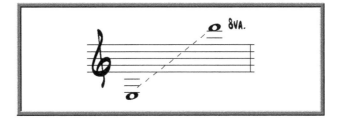

Notate the guitar on the treble clef only. Besides the use of only one staff, all the techniques for notating keyboards apply equally to guitar.

Bass

The electric and acoustic bass are transposing instruments, written one octave higher than they sound. Notate bass parts solely on bass clef. Some basses have a higher range than others, so the upper range can vary from concert B♭ above the top line of the bass clef to concert E directly above middle C (Examples 12.12 and 12.13.)

Example 12.12 Concert Range of the Bass

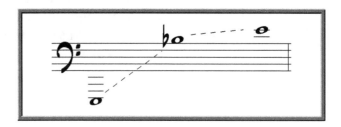

Example 12.13 Written Range of the Bass

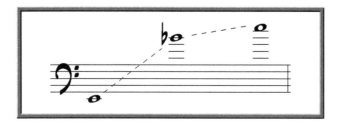

There are many nuances to notating bass parts that differ from the rest of the rhythm section. Bass charts may consist entirely of slashes, rhythmic slash notation, notation of specific pitches, or a combination of the three. In cases where notation of specific pitches is required, include the chord symbols as well.

Often a composer will have a specific bass line in mind for a song. The use of the word "simile" is a crucial element in such a case. Rather than notate the bass line throughout the entire song, the line can be written once with chord symbols above it, followed in the next measure or group of measures by slashes with chord symbols with the "simile" indication above them (Example 12.14.)

Example 12.14 Use of Simile in Bass Charts

153

An alternative method is the use of a 1- or 2-measure repeat symbol (Example 12.15.)

Example 12.15 Use of 2-measure Repeat in Bass Charts

When using 1- or 2-measure repeats or simile, notate the bass line at the beginning of each new section, as well as at the top of each new page. Do not use 4-measure repeats. In the case of a 4-measure bass line, the use of simile is preferred.

In bass charts consisting of a mixture of slashes and rhythmic notation, it is recommended that the beginning pitch of syncopated rhythms, especially anticipations, be incorporated into the notation (Example 12.16.)

Example 12.16 Rhythmic Notation of Syncopated Rhythms in Bass Charts

Of course, this method is only required when a <u>new</u> chord begins on a subdivision of a beat.

At times, it is necessary to include an additional notation of the style of bass line along with the groove indication of the song. For instance, there are several different styles of playing bass in a funk groove. There is the more conventional right-hand fingering style used by James Brown, as well as Tower of Power, and there is the right-hand slap fingering technique which began in the 1970's. Therefore, it is a good idea to include the word "slap" in parentheses next to the groove indication in the bass part.

Bass slap patterns can also be notated in a chart. There are two important elements in slap bass technique: 1.) The right-hand thumb hits or "slaps" the bass string, rather than plucks it, and then the player pulls it away immediately. 2.) One of the forefingers of the right hand, which plucks another string from below, pulling away and causing it to "pop". The palm or one of the fingers then quickly mutes the popped note. Notate this in a chart by indicating the slapped note with an "S" for slap above or below the note (Example 12.17.)

Example 12.17 Slap Bass Notation

The letter "P" can also be used to indicate popping, although this is rarely needed, as most bass players familiar with slap technique will naturally pop the correct notes. It is also a good idea to indicate at the beginning of the chart that "S = Slap," as not all bass players will be familiar with this style of notation.

There are also additional pop bass playing styles that require the use of the thumb or a pick rather than the forefingers. Indicate this at the beginning of the chart. In fact, the letter "T" can indicate the use of the thumb on specific notes if necessary. However, if the entire bass line is played with the thumb or pick, indicate it in parenthesis at the beginning of the chart or relevant section of the song.

It is difficult, however, for a bass player to switch between finger-style playing and the use of a pick in the middle of a song. In addition, such a switch may also require a different volume or tone setting by the bassist. Consequently, it is a good idea to work in several beats of rest before and after the section in which the bassist is to use a pick. Otherwise, it is perhaps best to settle on one or the other for the entire song. Switching between thumb- and finger-style playing, however, is not difficult.

There are several different types of bass lines in a swing groove. One style is the *two feel* swing style. In early jazz, from Dixieland to Big Band styles, bass players usually played in the two feel, or two-beat style. In fact, many modern society dance bands still play in this style. In a two feel, the drummer plays a 4/4 swing beat, but the bass player plays mostly half notes, usually outlining the root and 5th of each chord (Example 12.18.)

Example 12.18 Two Feel Bass Style

In Dixieland jazz style, this type of bass line is used, but the drums play a straight-8th-note groove, rather than a swing beat. In modern times, when a two feel is utilized, the bass player will often insert quarter-note major or minor 2nd passing tones leading to the next chord, making the bass line a bit more interesting, as illustrated in measure 2 of Example 12.19.

Example 12.19 Two Feel with Chromatic Passing Tones

Modern swing styles often consist of *walking* bass lines. A walking bass line is mostly quarter notes (or occasionally 8th notes,) outlining the chord or the scale. An early example of walking bass was the Boogie Woogie bass line in the early 20th Century (Example 12.20.)

Example 12.20 Boogie Woogie Walking Bass Line

The pianist often played the Boogie Woogie bass lines in the left hand, rather than a bass player. In fact, this is a rather difficult rhythm to play constantly on the bass. A similar bass line made up entirely of quarter notes was adopted in the swing era, and subsequently used extensively in rock-a-billy of the 1950's (Example 12.21.)

Example 12.21 Early Swing Jazz and Rock-a-billy Walking Bass Line

As in the boogie woogie bass line, it was standard to outline each chord in this way: 1-3-5-6-♭7-6-5-3. If the chart had a 6th chord, the bass player would play the root in place of the ♭7.

Beginning with the be-bop movement of the 1940's, jazz bassists began playing more adventurous walking bass lines, including more chromatic passing tones, and this type of walking bass line is still in use in modern jazz (Example 12.22.)

Example 12.22 Modern Jazz Walking Bass Line

In most cases, an indication of the bass style can be included along with the groove indication. The words "walk" or "2 feel" are generally adequate, and, depending on the groove indicated, the bass player will usually know which type of walking bass line to use.

Elements of a Walking Bass Line

A composer/arranger may wish to notate a specific walking bass line on occasion, so it is important to understand how walking bass lines function. There are several general rules for composing or playing walking bass lines:

- e Play the root at the beginning of each new chord.
- e Primary chord tones (root, 3rd, 5th and 7th) should be played on strong beats (1 and 3) whenever possible.
- e The final note of each chord should approach the root of the next chord by a major or minor 2nd whenever possible.

Incorporate swing 8th note rhythms (consisting of a quarter-note triplet followed by an 8th-note triplet) into a walking bass line to make it more rhythmically interesting. Simplify the notation of these rhythms by using a dotted 8th followed by a 16th note, or even two 8th notes. Indicate this at the beginning of the chart in the following way:

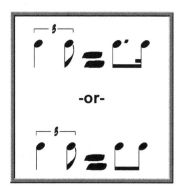

Figure 12.4 Swing rhythm Indications

The number of beats per chord may also affect the way a player approaches a walking bass line. Consider the following points with respect to the number of beats per chord (Lindsay, 1985.) Example 12.23 references the walking bass line over a standard 12-bar blues.

1) One beat per chord - the bass should play the root of each chord (measure 7)
2) Two beats per chord - the bass should play:
   a) The root, then 5th (or I5,) of each chord (measures 4, 7 and 12)
   b) The root followed by a note approaching the next chord root by a major or minor 2nd
   c) A combination of root to 5th and root to approach tone
3) Four beats per chord – the bass should play:
   a) The root to arpeggiated primary chord tones (measure 5)
   b) The root to octave root, followed by primary chord tones
   c) The root to arpeggiated chord tones to an approach tone on beat 4 (measure 6)
   d) A mixture of a and b, with a I5 on beat 4 (measures 1 and 8.)
   e) The root plus stepwise scale and chord tones; Beat 3 can be a primary chord tone or an extension, but not a chromatic passing tone, but beat 4 can be a chromatic passing tone (measures 2,3, and 9.) Blues scale movement is also acceptable on dominant 7th chords (measure 10.)
4) Eight beats or more per chord – the bass should play the root, followed by mostly stepwise motion, with primary chord tones on beat 1 of each measure, and primary chord tones or extensions on beat 3. In addition, incorporate elements from item number 3.

Example 12.23 Standard Walking Bass Line

Written Assignment 12.1: Compose a 16-measure bass line in 4/4 time, with chord symbols, in any musical style. The bass line must be at least four notes per measure, and one new chord per measure, with no note longer than a dotted quarter.

Drums

Notate the drum set on one staff, with a percussion clef (Example 12.24.)

Example 12.24 Drum Set Notation

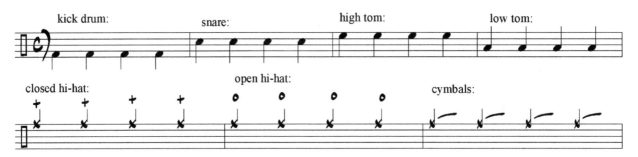

Each element of the drum set has it's own line or space on the staff, and drums are usually notated with normal note-heads, while cymbals use x note-heads. Example 12.25 illustrates a typical drum set pattern.

Example 12.25 Typical Drum Set Pattern

In most situations, it will not be necessary to notate a drum set chart as depicted in Example 12.25. Typically, a chart consisting of slashes and slash rhythmic notation without chord symbols will suffice. The groove indication will often give the drummer enough information to play the correct beat. However, some stylistic terms can be a bit vague, such as "rock". It can be beneficial to include the type of hi-hat pattern desired in such a situation. For instance, if the drummer is to play 8th notes on the hi-hat or ride cymbal, "8th note rock" would be an appropriate label. Likewise, if the drummer should play 16th notes on the hi-hat, indicate "16-note rock".

If a song is in 4/4, but the drum groove is more of a cut time feel, use the term "half-time feel". For example, a typical rock drum pattern will consist of the kick on beats 1 and 3 and the snare on beats 2 and 4. However, some songs have the same rhythmic drive, but the kick is on beat 1 and the snare is on beat 3 in each measure. Such a situation would require the use of the term "half-time feel". Similarly, there may be times in a song when a double-time feel is used. Rather than change the key signature or the tempo, the term "double-time feel" can be used.

Use of rhythmic notation is a bit different in a drum chart. Often the drummer will be required to accentuate a rhythm occurring in the other instruments. The arranger needs to make a decision as to whether or not the time or the groove should stop in these situations. If the drummer should stop keeping time and devote all of his or her energy to these rhythms, notate it with standard slash notation (Example 12.26.)

Example 12.26 Stopping Time to Play Rhythms

If, however, the composer/arranger wishes the drummer to keep the groove going, but accentuate the rhythms in addition, the slashes should remain with the rhythm notated above them (Example 12.27.)

Example 12.27 Groove with Rhythms Above

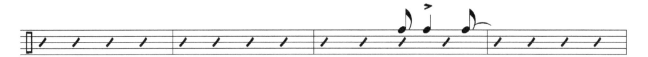

There are a number of lazy arrangers in the world who refuse to write drum charts, opting instead to make the drummer read a keyboard, bass, vocal or guitar part. Thus, drummers often get in the habit of playing through the rests. Consequently, whenever there is a section of rests in a drum chart, and the composer genuinely does not want the drummer to play, the word "tacet" should be placed above the first measure of rest. Tacet means "do not play".

Fills are often a part of a drum chart, so notate them in the same ways as other instruments. However, there may be times when the composer has a specific rhythm in mind for a fill. The composer can notate the rhythm exactly on the staff, including the correct combination of snare and toms. However, it is often better to notate the rhythm but leave the decision for the drum set fills to the individual drummer, as each drummer has a different playing style. Accomplish this by notating the rhythms without note-heads (Example 12.28.)

Example 12.28 Drum Fill Rhythm Notation Without Note-Heads

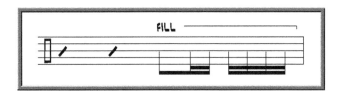

Improvised drum solos generally are played only in live performance, and are rarely incorporated into the studio versions of pop songs. However, there are times when an arranger may want to feature a drummer in a song. There are two basic types of drum solos: free-form solos and solos that are in time. Free-form solos are usually up to the drummer or the bandleader as to how long they will last. In addition, free-form solos usually stray from the basic tempo and beat of the song quite a bit. Then, it is up to the drummer to return to the beat of the song, if the song is supposed to continue. Notate a free-form solo in the following way (Example 12.29):

Example 12.29 Free-Form Drum Solo

The solo section should be in the same format in the other parts, with rests rather than slashes during the solo section, and the caption "drum solo (open)."

If the basic beat and tempo should not change during a drum solo, it is best to set a specific amount of time for the solo, using slashes (Example 12.30.)

Example 12.30 Drum Solo in Time

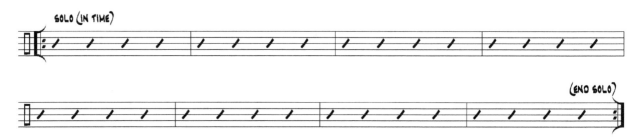

The words "in time" may not be necessary, but it is better to be safe. Place a multi-measure rest in the other parts, with the caption "drum solo (in time)".

Written Assignment 12.2: Write a drum chart for the 16 measure bass line composed in Assignment 12.1. Include at least one fill and one rhythmic accentuation matching a set of rhythms in the bass line.

Background Vocals

Arranging background vocals can be much more complicated than it would seem. Take a number of factors into account. The style of the song, the number of voices to be used, whether the background singers should be male, female, or both, and whether or not the song will be performed live or just recorded can all be important factors.

In a recording situation, for example, the lead singer may wish to sing all of the background vocals. However, the composer and/or the producer may feel that the background vocals should incorporate other voices. For instance, the lead singer may be male, and the composer may want female voices for the backgrounds, to get more of a 60's girl group sound. On the other hand, male voices singing in the upper range can be very powerful. Having a mixture of male and female voices can also produce distinctive sounds. The males can sing the lower harmonies and the females the higher harmonies, or a male and female voice can sing together on each note of the chord, producing a more androgynous sound.

The use or absence of vibrato in the vocal sound is also an important factor. Use of vibrato can give a background vocal more of a gospel or older R&B type of sound. However, if there are any classically trained singers in the group, this may taint the sound. A straight-tone sound in female voices, with the men singing straight-tone in head voice, can lend a more polished vocal jazz or jingle singer quality to the backgrounds. On the other hand, male voices belting in the higher ranges in straight-tone can be a very powerful sound.

Be sure to take into account the ranges of different voices. A note that is high in the male range can be low in the female range. Most singers can sing with more power in the high part of their range. Consequently, a lower female voice doubled by a male singing in the high part of his range will have more volume and power than the female voice alone would.

Composition of Background Vocal Harmonies

There are three different types of background vocals: 1.) Those providing harmony to the melody, moving in parallel motion or near-parallel motion, on the same lyric, 2.) Vocal pads made up of "oohs," "ahs," or a different set of lyrics, and 3.) "Call-and-response" vocals. In most pop songs, vocal harmonies consist of two- and three-part chords. Doubling the harmonies at the octave lends a gothic or operatic sound to the backgrounds.

Parallel harmonies will not always work; the chord changes should be relatively static, and even two chords per measure may be too much. The decision to use two- or three-part harmony must be made. If you are writing for a band with only two singers, then two-part harmony is the obvious choice. Once you have decided on two-part harmony, decide whether the harmony will be above or below the melody. Harmonies are more frequently above the melody in modern pop music, but this will also depend on the range of the background singer, as well as where the melody resides in relation to the chords. If the melody hovers around the 5th of the chord, the next harmony above it will be at the root, which means there will often be a perfect 4th between the two notes. In this situation, either a lower harmony or a higher harmony around the 3rd of the chord will be better.

If a three-part chord seems the better option, the arranger/composer must decide where the melody will be in relation to the harmonies. In many cases, both of the harmonies will be above the melody. However, putting the melody in the middle can also be effective, and if the melody is rather high, the two harmonies can be lower.

The note content of a parallel harmony line can also be problematic. The notes should conform to the scale or mode of the chord. Primary chord tones should be emphasized, and a line should usually begin and always end on a primary chord tone in each voice, in this case the root, 3rd and 5th. The 2nd, 4th, and 6th degrees are not absolutely forbidden, as long as the harmony does not dwell there too long. However, avoid the 7th unless the composer is seeking a "jazzy" sound.

Example 12.31 illustrates two three-part harmonies with the melody on the bottom, with two examples of each, one using all parallel motion but avoiding the 7th, and the other using less parallel motion.

Example 12.31 Two Sample Vocal Harmony Lines

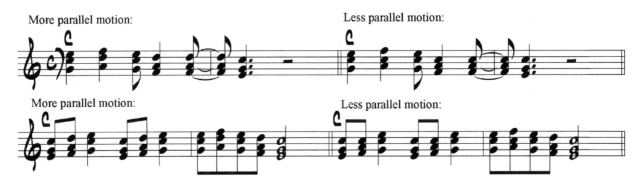

The first harmony in both examples is derived from gospel music. When the melody moves to another note, the harmony moves as well. In both of the second examples, maintain the root of the chord at all times, even when the other voices are not on primary chord tones.

An entire chapter or more could be written on the subject of parallel vocal harmony, for we have barely brushed on the subject. The most important point for the composer/arranger is: Above all, use your ears!

Vocal pads are much easier to compose, for they are independent of the melody. Vocal pads usually simply outline the chords, and they may reside in the same range as the melody, or in another range. They are usually most effective as three-part chords, although in certain cases, two-part chords will suffice. As mentioned above, sing them on a neutral syllable, such as "ooh", "oh", or "ah", or make up lyrics. However, take care so that the lyric in the vocal pad does not detract from the lyrics in the lead vocal.

Call-and-response background vocals are usually sung between lead vocal lines. They can add to the lyrical message, repeat a line sung by the lead vocalist, answer a question posed by the lead vocalist, or complete a lyrical phrase initiated by the lead vocalist. The responses can be in two or three parts, or even several singers in unison.

When to Use Background Vocals

Use background vocals with care. It is often wise to save the three-part harmonies for the chorus and the bridge. In fact, often a song will have no harmonies on the verses as well as the first chorus, followed by a two-part harmony on the second chorus, and a three-part harmony on the third chorus. In other cases, there may be two-part harmonies on all but the first one or two verses, and three-part harmonies on all of the choruses. Another option is no harmonies on the verses, two-part harmonies on the pre-choruses, and three-part harmonies on the choruses. In other words, use the vocal harmonies sparingly when possible, in order to help build to the climax of the song.

When recording background vocals, it is not uncommon to double, triple, and even quadruple each note. This gives the background vocals a very full sound, often unduplicated in live performance without using a choir or playing to tracks. If tracks are limited, the composer/arranger can often get away with overdubbing the top voice less than the rest of the voices, as the top voice will often intrinsically sound more powerful anyway.

Background Vocal Charts

Background vocal charts are typically much simpler than rhythm section charts. In fact, it is often possible to include the background vocals on the lead sheet, if they consist mostly of parallel harmony lines to the melody. If a separate chart is required, it can consist of one staff per system, if the harmonies are close. For male vocals, make a determination to use bass clef or treble clef. If the notes are in the higher male vocal range, requiring ledger lines in the bass clef, treble clef is preferred. Write male vocal harmonies, as well as lower female harmonies, transposed up an octave on the treble clef used for the tenor voice, as mentioned in chapter 3. It is interesting to note that this makes the tenor voice a transposing instrument!

A grand staff is only needed in cases where Beach Boys style harmonies are required, with the bottom voice singing low bass notes and the top voice singing high falsetto or soprano notes.

If the background vocals have a separate chart, it may contain many sections with multi-measure rests. However, it is a good idea to provide lyrical cues at the start of each new section, and the chord changes should be notated at least two measures before each new vocal entrance, so that the vocalists can easily find their first note. Notate the chord changes above the background vocal line as well, so that the vocalists have a pitch reference.

Written Assignment 12.3: Compose vocal harmonies for one of the melodies you have written previously for this class, with at least one harmony voice in parallel motion with the melody, for at least 16 measures.

Rhythm Section and Vocal Chart Checklist:

- ✓ Indicate instrument name and song title at the top of each page.
- ✓ First system on the first page is two inches from the top.
- ✓ Indicate tempo and/or groove marking in the beginning of the song.
- ✓ Use multi-measure rests between sections, if needed.
- ✓ Slashes are diagonal, and evenly spaced within the measure. Use a straight-edge.
- ✓ Bar lines at the beginning and end of each system
- ✓ Plan the form to make sure repeated sections will work, and every chart follows the same form.
- ✓ Plan measures ahead of time, and don't leave any space at the end of a system (unless you have staff paper where the staves cover the entire page)
- ✓ Keep your lyrics and chords as straight as possible; use a ruler underneath your lyrics to keep them straight
- ✓ Use staff paper with the staves far enough apart to accommodate lyrics and chord changes. Use 10- or 8-stave paper rather than 12-stave
- ✓ If using section letters, "A" should begin with the melody, after the introduction.
- ✓ Don't forget the use of "simile"
- ✓ Put each page on a separate sheet to reduce page turns; if you have multiple pages, you can tape them together.
- ✓ D.S. and Coda signs are easy to spot
- ✓ Fills and solo sections are clearly labeled
- ✓ Chord changes and vocal cues are included in the background vocal chart

Project 3: Write a pop song of at least 2 minutes, which includes background vocals and rhythm section. Provide written parts for rhythm section and background vocals, using as many of the elements discussed in this chapter as possible.

Checklist of Assignments for Chapter 12

- ✓ **Written Assignment 12.1:** Compose a 16-measure bass line in 4/4 time, with chord symbols, in any musical style. The bass line must be at least four notes per measure, and one new chord per measure, with no note longer than a dotted quarter.
- ✓ **Written Assignment 12.2:** Write a drum chart for the 16 measure bass line composed in Assignment 12.1. Include at least one fill and one rhythmic accentuation matching a set of rhythms in the bass line.
- ✓ **Written Assignment 12.3:** Compose vocal harmonies for one of the melodies you have written previously for this class, with at least one harmony voice in parallel motion with the melody, for at least 16 measures.
- ✓ **Project 3.0:** Write a pop song of at least 2:00 that includes background vocals and rhythm section. Provide written parts for rhythm section and background vocals, using as many of the elements discussed in this chapter as possible.

13

ADDITIONAL COMPOSITION TECHNIQUES

Riff-Based Composition

A riff is a repeating melodic or chordal pattern, often used as the basis for a composition. In cases where a song is not based on a riff, it may be used as a countermelody to the vocal line. Any melodic or harmonic instrument can play a riff, and the type of instrument often dictates how a riff is used. A riff can be anything from a single-note line to a series of chords married to a syncopated rhythm made up of quarter- eighth- and sixteenth-notes.

Chord Riffs

A chord riff is a repeating series of chords, usually moving in parallel motion with a syncopated rhythm. In other words, chord riffs are chord progressions notated with specific repeating rhythms, so rhythm is an integral component. Consequently, if notating a chord progression on a lead sheet using only slashes, rather than rhythmic notation, it is probably not a riff. In fact, it is often necessary to notate specific voicings for a chord riff. Example 13.1 illustrates a typical chord riff.

Example 13.1 Typical Chord Riff

The chords follow a specific syncopated rhythm, and each chord is a power chord with no 3rd. Each power chord has the same basic voicing, resulting in a series of ascending and descending parallel fifths. A guitar in "Drop D" tuning would play this riff.

Use a riff in many different ways in a song. Very few compositions consist entirely on riffs. Typically, only one or two sections of a song are riff-based. Use riffs in any part of a song, including verses, bridges, pre-choruses, choruses, and even intros, endings and interludes.

Single-Note or Melodic Riffs

A single-note or melodic riff is essentially a repeating monophonic series of notes. In traditional theory, this is an "ostinato". The term "melodic" in this context does not necessarily imply that the riff is a melody. In fact, a melodic riff often serves as accompaniment for the melody. All instruments can play his type of riff or one instrument can play it with the other instruments playing chords. Example 13.2 illustrates a typical melodic riff with a chord behind it:

Example 13.2 Melodic Riff Accompanied by a Chord

The song *Daytripper*, by the Beatles, uses a similar two-measure melodic riff. In the intro of *Daytripper*, the lead guitar plays the riff several times alone. Then, the bass joins in, followed by the rhythm guitar playing the E7 chord. The drums then enter, and finally the vocalist begins singing the melody, while the lead guitar continues playing the riff. As the song continues, the riff is sequenced up a perfect fourth (in measures 5 and 6 of the verse,) and the rhythm guitar plays an A7 chord. The riff is not played throughout the entire song. The chorus is comprised of a simple chord progression.

Daytripper is a classic case of a riff used as the basis for a song. Arguably, the riff of the song is in fact the hook, as it is perhaps more memorable than the melody. Furthermore, one can guess that Lennon and McCartney most likely composed the riff before they composed the melody. This is contrary to the traditional tenets of compositional practice, yet it is quite common in popular music.

Note that many guitar and keyboard riffs feature a combination of chord-based and melodic elements. *Sunshine of Your Love*, by Cream, and *Someone Saved My Life Tonight*, by Elton John both fit that category in different ways.
The two-measure guitar riff in Sunshine of Your Love begins as a melodic riff at the intro of the song. The third time the riff appears, however, the first four notes of the riff are chords in parallel motion. It is also interesting to note that this riff is based almost entirely on the D minor blues scale.

The piano riff in the intro of *Someone Saved My Life Tonight*, by Elton John, presents a different mixture of melodic and chord-based elements. The melodic riff is in the left hand, while the right hand plays rhythmically placed chords. As there is no parallel chord movement, this could technically be called a riff with chord accompaniment. Arguably, the chords in the right hand could be termed a pad. However, the two quarter notes played in the right hand at the beginning of each measure add rhythmic interest to the static half note in the left-hand riff. Therefore, the riff would not sound the same without the rhythmic impetus provided by the chords.

This particular riff exists only in the intro and the interludes between some sections of the song. The vocal melody is never sung concurrently with the riff. The hook of the song is the chorus, but the intro riff is also very memorable, constituting an additional hook.

169

In other words, a riff can be an integral component of a composition even if the verse, chorus or bridge does not feature it. Due to copyright restrictions, examples of the riffs discussed above could not be included in the text.

Examples of Guitar Riffs:

Black Dog and *Stairway to Heaven* by Led Zeppelin
Come As You Are by Nirvana
I Got You by James Brown
Layla by Derek & the Dominoes
Love Rollercoaster by The Ohio Players
Smoke On The Water by Deep Purple
Walk This Way by Aerosmith

Carry On Wayward Son by Kansas
Daytripper by the Beatles
Johnny B. Goode by Chuck Berry
Loser by Beck
Paranoid Android by Radiohead
Sunshine of Your Love by Cream
Wipeout by the Surfaris

Examples of Keyboard Riffs:

Stiletto by Billy Joel

Superstition by Stevie Wonder
Conga by Miami Sound Machine
Don't You Want Me by Human League
Jump by Van Halen

Someone Saved My Life Tonight and *Honky Cat* by Elton John
Feelin' Alright by Joe Cocker
She Blinded Me With Science by Thomas Dolby
1999 by Prince
You Make My Dreams Come True by Hall and Oates

Examples of Bass Riffs:

25 or 6 to 4 by Chicago
Roundabout by Yes
Another One Bites the Dust by Queen
Whip It! by Devo
Give It Away by The Red Hot Chili Peppers

Good Times by Chic
Fresh by Kool and the Gang
Dazed and Confused by Led Zeppelin
I Wish by Stevie Wonder
Fascination Street by The Cure

Examples of Horn (Brass and/or Woodwinds) Riffs:

Got To Get You Into My Life by The Beatles
Baker Street by Gerry Rafferty
What Is Hip by Tower of Power
Pick Up the Pieces by Average White Band

Sir Duke by Stevie Wonder
Jungle Boogie by Kool and the Gang
25 or 6 to 4 by Chicago

Examples of String Riffs:

I Am The Walrus and *Eleanor Rigby* by The Beatles
Livin' Thing by Electric Light Orchestra
Good Times by Chic

Written Assignment 13.1: Compose two riffs of at least two measures, for two different instruments.

Groove-Based Composition

A groove-based composition is a song based on a drum beat or groove. The groove will usually be the driving force of the song. Groove-based composition is riff-based composition for drums. However, the bass is often an integral component of the groove, and it plays a large part in many groove-based compositions.

In order to write a groove-based song, the composer must either be a drummer or have a good understanding of the drums. If the composer is not a drummer, he or she should have access to a drum machine or a sequencer with a multi-timbral synthesizer, in order to try out different drum grooves.

Sequencing Drum Parts

Sequencing drum parts can also be more difficult than it seems. Fortunately, there are many drum grooves available in General MIDI format, and a composer can take these and edit them in a sequencer to come up with the right groove. For those who are ambitious and want to try their hand at creating drum parts from scratch, an understanding of the physical aspects of playing the drums is required.

A typical drum beat will consist of a pattern alternating between the kick drum and the snare, accompanied by another rhythmic pattern, usually on the hi-hat or ride cymbal. Use the toms mostly for fills, and the crash cymbals (as well as the splash and the china cymbal) at the end of a fill or at the beginning of a phrase. A fill will often begin with the snare, and end with the floor tom or kick drum. However, play some fills entirely on the snare or the toms, or even a kick drum with a double bass pedal.

Drummers are human, and only have two arms, so they can only do two things at once with their hands. Use drumsticks to play the snare, toms, hi-hat (although there is a left foot component to this as well,) and crash and ride cymbals of the drum set.

In the course of a simple groove, with no fills, the drummer will play the snare with one hand (usually the left,) and either the hi-hat or the ride cymbal with the other. A common mistake among novice drum sequencers is to have an intricate hi-hat pattern, an intricate ride cymbal pattern, and the snare happening at the same time. This is physically impossible. The hi-hat can be closed with the foot pedal while the drummer is playing the ride cymbal, but this can only be done in quarter notes at best. In addition, the sound of a hi-hat with the pedal is less crisp than the sound of a closed hi-hat played by a stick. Most multi-timbral modules and drum machines will have two different closed hi-hat sounds, and you should determine which is the pedal sound and which is the stick sound.

The hi-hat itself has a surprising array of different sounds. There is the sound of the pedal without the use of a drumstick, and the sound of a closed hi-hat hit by a drumstick, as mentioned above. There is also the sound of the open hi-hat struck with the stick, then closed immediately after. This gives a sharp attack, followed by a short sustain, then a quick percussive release. A hi-hat pattern will often consist of a mixture of the closed hi-hat strike and the open-to-closed hi-hat strike. An additional sound is that achieved when the drummer loosens the top cymbal of the hi-hat, so that it cannot raise any more. When the drummer strikes the hi-hat, it has a sharp attack with a muted sustain as the two cymbals vibrate against each other. This sound, of course, cannot be alternated with the fully open hi-hat, because the drummer can no longer open the hi-hat.

A hi-hat or ride cymbal pattern will usually cease when a fill is played, as it usually takes two hands to play a fill. However, the hi-hat can be played using the pedal during a fill, although not all drummers can do this very well. Remember that hi-hat patterns utilizing 8th-note or 16th-note rhythms require the use of two hands, so the snare pattern is usually relatively simple. The ride cymbal is played with one hand, and 8th-notes are usually the shortest rhythms that can be played consistently. Remember also that when playing the crash cymbal at the end of a fill or beginning of a phrase, the hi-hat and ride will usually stop shortly.

Another common mistake made by novice drum sequencers is misuse of the kick drum. The kick drum will generally match some of the rhythms in the bass line. However, the kick does not usually match the entire bass line note-for-note. Typically, the kick drum rhythms are rather spare, usually playing on beat 1, then resting, and then playing on beat 3 or some other rhythmic subdivision of beat 2 or 3. A kick drum may only play two notes in a typical measure, and sometimes 3 or 4. A drummer in some punk and metal styles may play sustained 16th note rhythms on a kick drum fitted with a double bass pedal. Note that the use of both feet makes an open-to-closed hi-hat sound impossible.

When sequencing a drum part, it is best to start with the kick and snare, playing an alternating rhythm between the two. Then add the hi-hat or ride cymbal. It is probably best to fill in the basic groove of the entire song before adding fills. If there is one groove used throughout the song, copy and paste a 2- or 4-measure pattern until the sequence reaches the desired number of measures. Then, you can go back in and add fills, making sure to edit out any hi-hat and ride cymbal notes, as well as kick and snare notes, which may conflict with the fills.

Composing a Groove-Based Song

As mentioned above, the bass line is often as integral to the groove as the drum pattern. In fact, a certain drum groove may inspire a certain bass line, and vice versa. It is not uncommon, then, to compose the drum groove and the bass line first, write chords to the bass line, then the melody to that. Alternatively, compose the melody to the drum groove and bass line, and the combination of bass line and melody will suggest the harmonies. It is best to experiment, and find which method suits you.

Note that many groove-based compositions are composed of riffs as well, and these two compositional techniques often go hand-in-hand.

Examples of Groove-Based Songs:

- e   Walk This Way by Aerosmith
- e   Life's Been Good by Joe Walsh
- e   These Shoes by The Eagles
- e   We Will Rock You by Queen
- e   Rock and Roll, Part Two by Gary Glitter
- e   In The Air Tonight by Phil Collins
- e   Squibcakes by Tower of Power

Sample-Based Composition

Sample-based composition is a new phenomenon, and is a form of groove-based or riff-based composition. A composer or producer will take a sampled (digitally recorded) groove or riff from a previously recorded song by another artist, and use it as the basis for a new composition. This type of composition originated in hip-hop and dance music, but it has found it's way into mainstream pop music in recent years.

There are a number of different approaches to sample-based composition. For instance, a 2-to-4-measure drum groove may be sampled and looped, and a new bass line and chord changes composed to the groove. Then, a melody or rapped lyrics are set to that. Alternatively, the sample may consist of harmonic material from a song, with a new drum groove added underneath. In recent years, artist/producers such as Puff Daddy have sampled entire songs and written new lyrics to them.

In the early years of sampling, many critics decried it as lacking in artistic integrity. However, over the years, many artists have used samples in unique and ingenious ways, thus gaining a measure of respect, or at least acceptance, by musicians and critics alike.

Project 4.0: Compose a song based on at least one riff and/or groove. Write a lead sheet and parts for rhythm section.

Checklist of Assignments for Chapter 13

- ✓ **Written Assignment 13.1:** Compose two riffs of at least two measures, for two different instruments.
- ✓ **Project 4.0:** Compose a song based on at least one riff and/or groove. Write a lead sheet and parts for rhythm section.

14

ARRANGING FOR BRASS AND WOODWINDS

Brass and woodwinds, alone or in combinations, are frequently in popular music. Many pop compositions feature an individual instrument playing riffs and/or an improvised solo. Perhaps the most often used are the alto and tenor saxophone, and in recent years, the soprano saxophone. However, over the years, there were songs featuring the trumpet and flugelhorn, flute, and even the trombone.

A horn section, usually consisting of trumpet, trombone, alto and tenor saxophones, is quite common as well. A horn section will generally play a mixture of riffs, pads, and percussive stabs. Some lines may consist of melodic riffs in unison or octave unison, and some are chord riffs.

Certain musical styles tend to feature horn sections more frequently than others do. Jazz Rock is the most obvious, with bands such as Chicago and Blood, Sweat and Tears. Many Funk and Disco Bands, such as Earth, Wind and Fire, Kool & the Gang, and Tower of Power have horn sections. The Tower of Power horn section includes a baritone saxophone player. A number of Ska bands also have horn sections, and some of them only consist of trumpets and trombones.

Of course, the popular music of the 1930's was big band music, and the typical big band may contain four or five trumpets and trombones, two tenor and alto saxophones, and a baritone saxophone. In addition, some big bands contained other wind instruments, such as the clarinet. There are entire volumes devoted to the art of arranging for big band, and the subject is much too complicated to cover here. We will instead concentrate on the small horn sections and solo instruments used in modern pop music.

First, it is important to understand the range and transposition of each instrument, as well as their sonic characteristics.

Brass Instruments

Brass instruments tend to have a bright, "brassy" sound, with a wide dynamic range. It is actually easier for a brass player to play loud sounds than soft sounds, believe it or not.

Trumpet

The trumpet is the lead instrument in the horn section. Lead trumpet players are usually capable of playing very high notes at a loud dynamic level that carries over the rest of the horn section. In a big band setting, the lead trumpet will often play the melody, with the other trumpets and the rest of the band playing lower harmonies. In a small horn section, the trumpet will also play the top notes.

The trumpet is a transposing instrument, written up a major 2nd from concert pitch, and notated on the treble clef. Example 14.1 illustrates the concert and written range of the trumpet.

Example 14.1 Trumpet Range

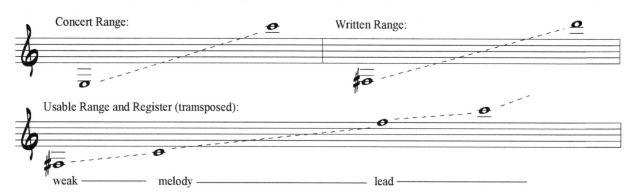

The low range of the trumpet can be rather weak, and it is more difficult to play loud. Conversely, in the lead range, soft sounds are more difficult to play.

The flugelhorn is the cousin of the trumpet. The usable range of the flugelhorn is lower than that of the trumpet, and it has a much more mellow sound. Flugelhorn is also a transposing instrument. Like the trumpet, it is written up a major 2nd from concert pitch, and notated on the treble clef. Example 14.2 illustrates the written range of the flugelhorn.

Example 14.2 Flugelhorn Range (Transposed)

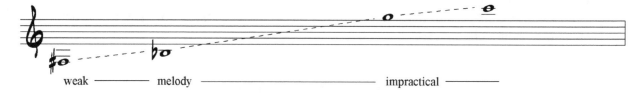

Flugelhorn is often used for solo or unison lines, and two flugelhorns playing a unison riff are quite common. However, flugelhorn is not often used in horn sections playing chords, and high notes are often difficult.

Trombone

The trombone is one of the lower brass instruments. It is capable of playing low bass notes, as well as higher notes. The trombone is a nontransposing instrument, and is notated on the bass clef. The tenor trombone is the most commonly used trombone (Example 14.3.)

Example 14.3 Tenor Trombone Range

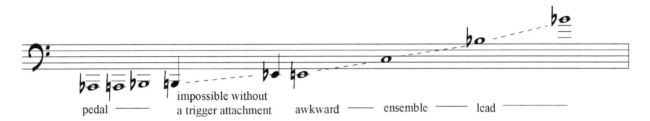

The "pedal" notes, pictured at the beginning of the measure, are low notes played with an extremely loose embouchure (i.e., very loose lips.) These notes can often be played at a loud volume, but it is difficult to play a series of pedal notes very fast. The standard tenor trombone, with no trigger attachments, has a gap between pedal Bb and the Eb below the bass clef, in which notes are impossible. However, a tenor trombone with a trigger attachment, which contains extra tubing, can hit these notes. When the trigger is pressed, the sound routs to the extra tubing, and additional notes are possible. Not all tenor trombone players own horns with trigger attachments, so it is better to avoid these notes.

The trombone uses a slide rather than valves (although valve trombones do exist,) so it is more difficult to play fast lines in the lower register. 8th- and 16th-note lines are easier in the ensemble register and much easier in the lead register. However, not all trombone players are comfortable playing in the lead register.

Of course, an important feature of the trombone is the ability to play long glissandos (sliding from one note to another) and fall-offs (sliding down after a note has been played.) A smooth glissando of a perfect 4th can be played from F below the staff to Bb, the C above that to F, and F to Bb above the staff (Example 14.4.)

Example 14.4 Trombone Glissando

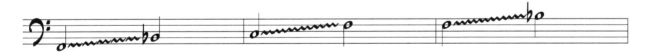

The bass trombone has a larger bell and mouthpiece than the standard tenor trombone, as well as at least one trigger attachment. It is capable of playing low notes with more volume and depth, but it is more difficult to play high notes. The bass trombone is for bass notes, but it can play lower ensemble parts as well. It is a nontransposing instrument (Example 14.5.)

178

Example 14.5 Bass Trombone Range

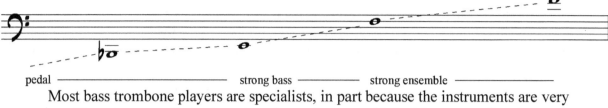

pedal ——————————————— strong bass —————— strong ensemble ——————————

Most bass trombone players are specialists, in part because the instruments are very expensive. Do not assume that a tenor trombone player could double very well on bass trombone.

Woodwind Instruments

The woodwind family of instruments is very diverse, and some are capable of a wide range of sounds. The saxophones are probably the most versatile, especially the alto, tenor and baritone saxes. These instruments can play loud, bright tones that blend well with brass instruments, or soft, mellow tones. Of course, a saxophone, which is made of metal, cannot produce a tone as mellow as a wood clarinet.

The woodwind instruments we will deal with here are the saxophones and the flutes, as modern pop music includes many of these instruments. The clarinet, although quite popular over 50 years ago, rarely appears in today's popular music. Note that many woodwind players are capable of playing more than one woodwind instrument (this is often called "doubling,") as most of them have identical or similar fingerings. Also, note that all of the saxophones (even the baritone) appear on the treble clef.

Soprano Saxophone

The soprano saxophone has become rather popular in recent years, due to artists such as Sting and Kenny G. Composers use it as solo instrument rather than an ensemble instrument. The soprano is the highest of the saxophones, and is transposed up a major 2nd from concert pitch (Example 14.6.)

Example 14.6 Soprano Saxophone Range

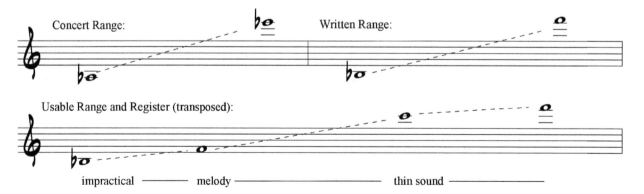

impractical ——— melody ————————————— thin sound ———————

The melody range of the soprano saxophone is the most effective register, and it is best to stay within this range.

The alto saxophone is often the lead instrument in a saxophone section. Transpose it up a major 6th from concert pitch (Example 14.7.)

Example 14.7 Alto Saxophone Range

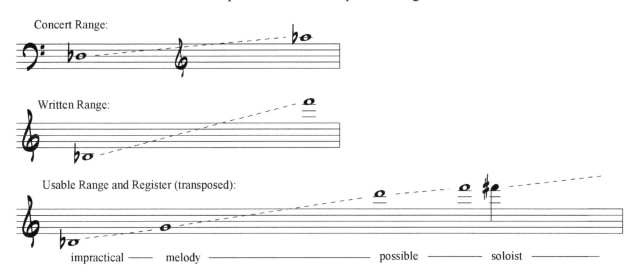

Once again, it is best to stay within the melody range in an ensemble setting. Soloists often play the notes higher than written D above the staff, but it is not a good idea to use these notes in an ensemble setting, as not all players can hit them. The low register between written Bb below the staff and G on the second line is usually rather weak. Alto saxophone solos are quite common in Rock and older Rhythm and Blues.

The tenor saxophone is a rather versatile instrument. It can play almost as low as the tenor trombone (excluding the pedal notes,) yet it can reach into the higher range as well. Generally, the entire range of the instrument is useful. The tenor saxophone is transpose up a major 9th (an octave plus a major 2nd) from concert pitch (Example 14.8.)

Example 14.8 Tenor Saxophone Range

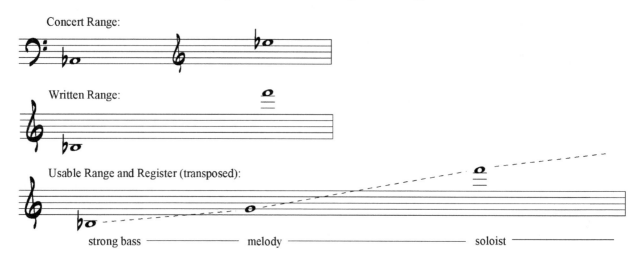

Tenor saxophone solos occur frequently in pop music. The baritone saxophone is the bass instrument of the saxophone family. It possesses a very strong bass register, and the higher range of the instrument can be used for ensemble parts. Transpose the baritone sax up a major 13th (an octave plus a major 6th) from concert pitch (Example 14.9.)

Example 14.9 Baritone Saxophone Range

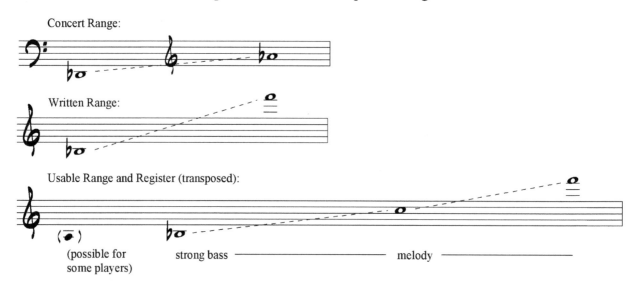

The baritone saxophone most often plays low bass notes, often in tandem with the bass trombone. Baritone sax solos are extremely rare in pop music, but a few examples exist.

When arranging for saxophones, it is helpful to remember the following: The different transpositions of the saxophones are such that the written (transposed) range for all four is the same, from Bb below middle C to F an octave above the staff (Example 14.10.)

Example 14.10 Written Range of All Saxophones

Example 14.11 illustrates the concert ranges of the four saxophones.

Example 14.11 Concert Ranges of Saxophones

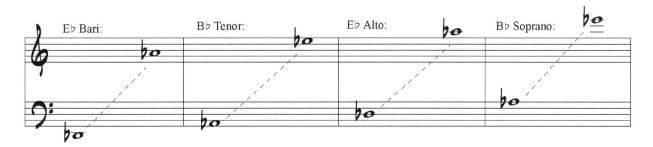

The flute is one of the highest woodwinds, and functions in pop music mostly as a solo instrument or in combination with another instrument. The flute is nontransposing, and is notate on the treble clef (Example 14.12.)

Example 14.12 Flute Range

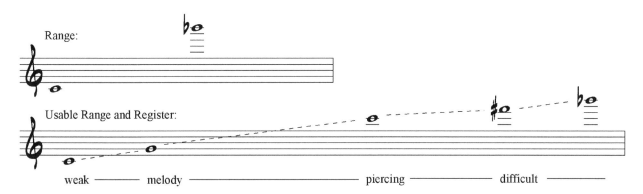

The register above the melody range is rarely used, except in some ensemble settings and improvised solos. At the end of this chapter is a quick reference chart with the transpositions, concert and written ranges of each instrument.

Written Assignment 14.1: Transpose the melody for each instrument, including the proper key signature, clef and transposed chord symbols.

Writing Brass and Woodwind Charts

Many of the arranging techniques for rhythm section (Chapter 11) apply to horn parts as well. One of these is the use of articulations, which function in the same way for brass and woodwinds. Improvised solo sections should include the chord changes, and they must conform to the transposition of the instrument. For instance, if the trumpet has an improvised solo, transpose the chord changes up a major 2nd. The chord changes do not need to be included in the rest of the chart. The format of a horn chart is the same as that of a rhythm section chart, and multi-measure rests are treated the same way. Refer to the rhythm section chart checklist at the end of Chapter 11 when writing horn charts.

A very important ingredient of a horn chart is dynamic markings. Rhythm section charts do not usually include dynamic markings, but they are integral to horn parts. Classical music and pop music both use the dynamic markings ("p" for soft, "f" for loud, etc.). Brass and woodwind players expect to see dynamic markings so do not overlook this.

Choice of key for a song featuring horn section can be crucial as well. Brass and woodwind players often prefer flat keys (in concert pitch, that is.) Guitar keys such as E are more difficult, especially for brass players. That does not mean that sharp keys are impossible, but you may have to listen to quite a few complaints.

Characteristic Horn Section Devices

Earlier in the chapter, we mentioned *falloffs*. A line curving downward from the note head indicates falloffs. Example 14.13 illustrates a long note with a sforzando-piano and crescendo, followed by a short accented note with a falloff.

Example 14.13 Falloff

Another device used in horn parts is the *Scoop*. Scoops are typically used in unison riffs, although they can be used with chords as well. To play a scooped note, the horns will usually begin a minor 2nd below the note and quickly slide up to the pitch. Scoops are, of course, easier for trombones, but the other instruments can usually use their embouchure to slide up to the note. Typically, the player will scoop only one or two notes in a riff. It is rather difficult to scoop an entire series of notes. Example 14.14 illustrates the scoop indication on the first and third notes.

Example 14.14 Scoops

Yet, another common device is the *Shake*. A shake only works on notes with a value of a quarter note or longer. It is similar to the trill in classical music. Play the note and then alternate it with a note a major 2nd or more above it, at least several times. On notes longer than a half-note, the note will sound for a moment, then the shake will begin, starting slow and speeding up as the end of the note nears. On shorter notes, the shake commences as soon as the artist initiates the note. Indicate a shake with a wavy line above the note (Example 14.15.)

Example 14.15 Shakes

If the horns are playing a voiced chord, often the lead trumpet is the only instrument performing the shake. On a unison line, however, all the instruments should shake. Shakes work best on brass instruments in the higher registers. If a horn section consists only of saxes, the shake may end up sounding too much like a classical trill.

Mutes are very effective devices for brass instruments. A Harmon mute is an aluminum mute, which gives the brass instrument a soft, metallic tone. Trumpets use these devices the most often. A cup mute gives the instrument a soft, mellow tone. A plunger mute is a rubber toilet plunger without the handle. The instrumentalist holds the plunger in his/her hand, covering and uncovering the bell at different times. This produces a characteristic "wah wah" sound in a brass instrument. The symbols used to indicate an open and closed hi-hat in drum notation also indicate an open and closed plunger in brass notation.

Use of mutes should be indicated at the beginning of the relevant section (for instance, "Harmon mute",) and it should also be indicated when the mute is to be taken out ("end Harmon mute.") Allow brass players at least one measure of rest before and after a muted section, to allow them to insert or remove the mute.

Riffs and Chords in Horn Section Charts

As mentioned previously, a horn chart will generally consist of a mixture of melodic and chord riffs, pads, and stabs. Use unison and chord riffs as fills, in between phrases in the melody. A typical technique is to begin with a unison riff that breaks into a chord riff on the last few notes. Stabs are also usually used as fills, but they generally occur more frequently, at times even in the middle of a vocal phrase. Pads can often be played while the vocalist is singing.

There may also be a horn section soli that features the horns. A soli will typically consist of melodic and chord riffs interspersed with stabs, but probably no pads. Composed in the style of an improvised solo, a soli features the trumpet or another lead instrument playing the melody, with the harmonies below it. If you listen to practically any song by Chicago or Blood Sweat and Tears from the late 1960's through the '70's, you will notice a common format of their solis. They would typically begin in the low registers, using mostly unison riffs with an occasional chord here and there. Near the end of the soli, the instruments were playing in the higher registers, using chord riffs and repeated stabs.

Chord Voicings in Three-Part Harmony

Voicing of chords in a pop song for a horn section is not as easy as it would seem, even though most of the chords are two- or three-part chords. We will look at a typical pop horn section with one trumpet, alto sax, tenor sax, and tenor trombone. The most typical order of the voices is: the trumpet on top, followed by the alto sax, tenor sax, and trombone. Of course, the alto sax is capable of playing the top part, but it is more common for the trumpet to take the lead.

In a two-part chord, the trumpet and alto sax should play the upper part, and the tenor sax and trombone the lower part. However, if the lower part is high, the trombone may have to double the trumpet at the octave. Then the tenor sax will play the lower part, and the alto sax will double either the trumpet or the tenor sax. Doubling the tenor sax may be the preferred option, since the trombone is already doubling the trumpet.

In a three-part chord (i.e., a triad,) things get a bit more complicated. If the trumpet is in the low-to-middle register, voice a chord in closed position, with the trombone either doubling the tenor sax in unison or doubling the trumpet down an octave. With the trumpet in the higher registers, however, use an open position *drop 2* chord. This is an example of a spread voicing. In a drop 2 chord voicing, the note that would normally be directly below the top voice is transposed down an octave to one of the lower voices. Example 14.16 illustrates a second-inversion C triad in closed position, and drop 2.

Example 14.16 Drop 2 Voicing

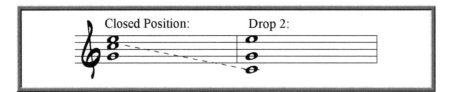

In this configuration, the trombone would play the second voice down an octave, the tenor would play the third voice, and the alto would double the trumpet or tenor sax. Alternatively, the trumpet, alto, and tenor could play the first, second and third voice respectively, and the trombone could double the second voice, or alto sax, down an octave. We might call this a "Closed Position Drop 2", and it would fill out the chord very well (Example 14.17.)

Example 14.17 "Closed Position Drop 2" Voicing

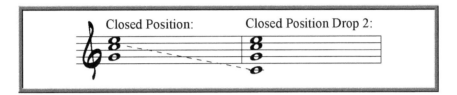

7 Important Rules for Voicing Chords in Three or More Voices:

1. No more than a minor 7th interval between adjacent voices. The only time this rule can be broken is when the bottom voice is playing low bass notes.
2. When there is a major 2nd between two middle voices, the voices on either side should be at least a minor 3rd away.
3. When there is a minor 2nd between two voices, the intervals above and below should be no larger than a tritone.
4. Avoid 2nds between the top two voices. Minor thirds and larger are usually better.
5. In a spread voicing, it is generally preferable to have smaller intervals between the top two voices, and the larger intervals between the lower voices.
6. Avoid intervals of a ♭9 between any two voices, except in a dominant 7 ♭9 chord.
7. Avoid seconds and thirds between adjacent voices below the E♯ on the third space of the bass clef.

Two-Part Harmony

Two-part harmony is generally most effective with a series of connected notes, rather than stabs or held notes. When harmonizing a note in two parts, it is best to place the lower note a diatonic 3rd or 6th below the top voice. Avoid using the root and 5th of the chord together, with no 3rd. If the top note is the root or 5th of the chord, the bottom note should be written as the 3rd, and if the top note is the 3rd, the bottom note should be written as the 5th. The 3rd and 7th can be used together in a 7th chord, but it is only recommended for stabs, and should be avoided in a connected note series. An interval of a 4th or 5th between two moving lines often produces an undesirable sound.

Harmonizing 7th Chords in Four Parts

When harmonizing 7th chords, the arranger can take advantage of jazz arranging techniques. One such technique is the use of *7th Chord Tone Categories*. A 7th chord has four elements: The root, 3rd, 5th, and 7th, and these are the categories we use to harmonize a 7th chord. In order to make the voicings more interesting, and to solve any voice leading problems that may occur in harmonizing a melodic line, some of the categories include alternative extensions.

The 3rd and 7th categories should always be filled in with the 3rd and 7th of the chord. However, there are two exceptions: The ♯4 will replace the 3rd on a sus4 chord, and the ♯6 can be substituted for the 7th in a major 7th chord. The root can be replaced by the 9th, and the 5th can be replaced by the 11th or 13th. These extensions can be altered, if they are specified in the chord symbol. However, if the chord symbol for the 7th chord does not include an extension, use the extension in its natural or altered form. If you do alter an extension in your voicing, it is wise to change the chord symbol to include this alteration.

Follow the seven rules for voicing chords on the previous page when voicing 7th chords. For instance, if using the 13th in a dominant 7th chord, do not voice the 13th in the octave below the 7th, for an interval of a minor 9th will occur. Table 14.1 lists the four chord tone categories for 7th chords with the chord tones and extensions included in each chord.

Table 14.1 7th Chord Tone Categories

Category	Chord Tone/Extension
Root	Root, ♭9, ♮9, ♯9
3rd	♭3, ♮3, (♮4 in a sus4 chord)
5th	♮11, ♯11/♭5, ♮5, ♯5/♭13, ♮13
7th	♭7, ♮7, (♮6 on major 7th chord)

Table 14.2 illustrates the best extensions to use for each chord category.

Table 14.2 Available Extensions for 7th Chords

Category	Major 7	Dominant 7	Minor 7	Minor 7♭5
Root	♮9	♭9, ♮9, ♯9	♮9	♮9
3rd	(♮4 on sus4 chord)	(♮4 on sus4 chord)	--	--
5th	♯11, ♭13	♯11, ♭13, ♮13	♭11	♭11
7th	♮6	--	--	--

Always use the ♮6 in the 7th category when the root is in the lead on a major 7th chord.
7th chords can be voiced in either closed position or drop two. Two other options for 7th chords is the drop 3 voicing, where the third voice from the top is transposed down an octave, and drop 2 & 4, in which the second and fourth voice are dropped down an octave (Example 14.18.)

Example 14.18 Drop 2, Drop 3, and Drop 2 & 4 Voicings

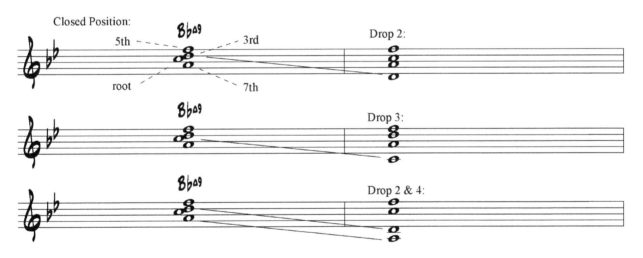

Written Assignment 14.2: Harmonize notes in closed position, drop 2, drop 3 and drop 2 & 4.

Composing a Riff or Soli

Compose a riff or soli section using the melodic devices discussed in Chapter 10. In addition, it is a good idea to integrate some stabs into the riff or soli, as this has great dramatic effect. Example 14.19 illustrates a riff with some stabs integrated into it.

Example 14.19 Horn Riff with Stabs

Note that the last stab includes a falloff. Falloffs are very effective with stabs. The stabs pictured here can be harmonized or in unison. It is up to the composer.

In addition to stabs, the riff can contain some notes longer than a quarter note. These will give the composer better opportunities for harmonizing chords. For notes longer than a half note, incorporate a change of dynamic level, such as a crescendo or a decrescendo.

The harmonic materials drawn on in devising horn riffs can sometimes differ from those used in a typical melody. Even in a pop context, horn sections often draw material from jazz influences. Blues and Bebop scales add an element of chromaticism to a scalewise motive. These scales are frequently used for 7th chords, but they will fit many triadic harmonies as well.

Another common element of horn riffs is arpeggiation of chords, either in a series of connected notes or stabs.

Harmonizing Riffs or Soli Melodies for Horn Section

Harmonizing a riff or the melody of a soli can also be a bit tricky. First, remember that the top voice is usually the melody. You can put the melody in a lower voice, but it is not always as effective. The most important rule is: whenever the top voice moves, the lower voices should move as well, using the same intervals whenever possible. In other words, try to avoid repeated notes in the lower voices, unless the top voice is repeating a note. All of the voices should move in roughly parallel motion.

First, write out the riff or melody with the chord changes above it. Play through the riff/melody several times. Make a decision as to which parts of the melody should be in unison, which should be in two parts, and which should be in four parts. The easiest approach is to look at each motive of the riff.

The following are some general concepts that will help in determining whether to use unison or harmony:

e Stabs and notes a quarter note or longer are usually best harmonized in three or four parts.

e Motives consisting of a series of scalewise adjacent 8th- or 16th-notes are often harmonized in two parts or unison.

e Motives that are lower in the register of the lead instrument may lend themselves better to unisons or two-part chords.

e Motives made up of leaps sound great in three- or four-part harmony, but if the motive starts in the low register, you may wish to begin in two parts.

e Motives containing chromatic notes may be difficult (though not impossible) to harmonize in three or four parts

e Motives can begin in unison or unison octaves, and then break into harmony. This may be beneficial especially if the motive begins in a low register and moves up.

e An option is to follow the contour of the melody, using unisons in the low range, two-part chords in the mid-range, and three- or four-part chords in the high range. However, a three-octave unison with the lead on high notes can be very powerful as well.

When moving between unison and harmony, expect that not all the voices would move in the same direction. Some will move up and some will move down. Once you have determined which parts will be in unison, two and three parts, there are a few other things to think about with regard to harmony voices:

e Melody notes in the higher register should generally be harmonized with an open voicing, while low notes should be in a closed voicing

e In two-part harmony of motives made up of sequential notes, the two parts should generally be either a 3rd or 6th apart.

e Remember to use as few repeated notes as possible, except when there are repeated notes in the melody.

In the sections you plan to harmonize in three or four voices, check for primary chord tones. Then, fill in the chord tones in the voices below. Do this first, so that you can determine the best methods of voice-leading into the chords. You must try to avoid too many large leaps in the individual voices.

Passing Chords

When harmonizing the melody in scalewise lines, harmonize any notes that are not primary chord tones with passing chords. Passing chords usually fall on weak beats, but they can fall on a strong beat as long as the next chord contains primary chord tones. It is best to avoid passing chords on beat one, however, unless the next chord consists of primary chord tones and is a quarter note or longer. Typically, you should only use one passing chord at a time between primary chords. However, two or more passing chords in a row may be unavoidable at times.

When harmonizing a passing chord, concentrate on the next chord rather than the chord preceding it. There are two types of passing chords: Diatonic Passing Chords and Parallel Passing Chords. Diatonic passing chords will contain extensions of the applicable chord scale. The note in each lower voice will approach the next by a major or minor 2nd, depending on the chord scale. For instance, if the melody note approaches the next by a major 2nd, the other voices may approach by either a major 2nd or minor 2nd, depending on the chord scale (Example 14.20.)

Example 14.20 Diatonic Passing Chord

Parallel passing chords are chords in which all of the voices approach the next chord using the exact interval used in the lead. This will result in one or more accidentals (Example 14.21.)

Example 14.21 Parallel Passing Chord

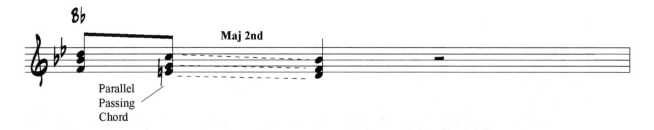

Chromatic passing tones in the lead will usually require parallel passing chords, and often they will require the use of two or more passing chords in a row. In such a situation, the arranger may wish to use parallel passing chords or a mixture of parallel and diatonic passing chords. Example 14.22 illustrates the use of a diatonic passing chord followed by a parallel passing chord.

Example 14.22 Diatonic Passing Chord Followed by a Parallel Passing Chord

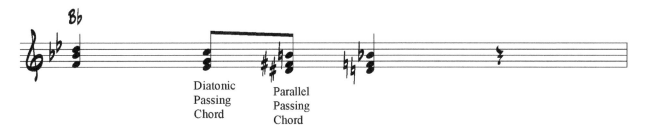

Diatonic
Passing
Chord

Parallel
Passing
Chord

In Example 14.22 above, the lowest voice is an E♭ in the first passing chord, followed by a D♯ in the second, the same note with a different enharmonic spelling. This breaks the rule of using no repeated notes. If both chords are parallel passing chords, the problem is solved (Example 14.23.)

Example 14.23 Two Parallel Passing Chords

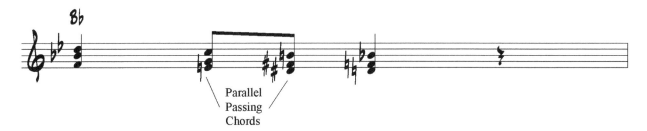

Parallel
Passing
Chords

The method in Example 14.23 solves the problem, creating movement in all of the voices. When using a series of two or more parallel passing chords, it is important to play through the voicings with the chord underneath, making sure it sounds good. If there are more than two passing chords in a row, you may need to use some diatonic passing chords, even if it means repeated notes. Otherwise, the passing chords may end up sounding too far out of the key.

Use passing chords even if the note is preceded by a leap, followed by a step. Use either a diatonic passing chord (Example 14.24) or parallel passing chord (Example 14.25) in this instance.

Example 14.24 Diatonic Passing Chord Preceded by a Leap

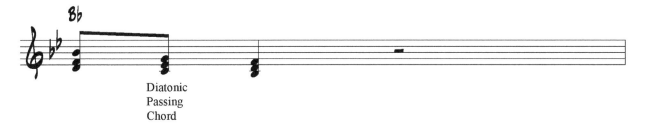

Diatonic
Passing
Chord

Example 14.25 Parallel Passing Chord Preceded by a Leap

Parallel
Passing
Chord

On occasions where a non-chord tone is followed by a leap, you can usually harmonize it as a diatonic passing chord, but use the preceding chord as your guide, rather than the following chord (Example 14.26.)

Example 14.26 Diatonic Passing Chord Followed by a Leap

Diatonic
Passing
Chord

Note that all the voices move by a 2nd from the preceding chord, rather than by a 4th to the following chord. When the non-chord tone is a chromatic note, the same method can be used, but with a parallel passing chord (Example 14.17.)

Example 14.27 Parallel Passing Chord Followed by a Leap

Parallel
Passing
Chord

If a non-chord tone is preceded and followed by a leap, a similar approach can be taken. However, it is also possible to use unison or unison octaves in order to avoid it. Passing chords are also very effective for background vocals and keyboard riffs. If you are harmonizing a line where the chord symbol is a 7th chord, remember to use extended chords as well. For instance, a D♮ in the melody over a C7 chord can be voiced as a C9 chord. This can help eliminate too many passing chords if needed.

Written Assignment 14.3: Harmonize the 4-measure melody in the workbook, using a combination of unison/unison octave, two parts, three parts, and four parts.

Additional Woodwind and Brass Instrument Combinations

Several less conventional combinations of instruments can be very effective in pop music. We have already discussed the use of two flugelhorns playing in unison. Another frequently used combination is a trumpet (or flugelhorn) playing in unison with a flute. A trumpet with a Harmon mute in unison with a flute is commonly used as well. Additionally, two or more trumpets playing voiced chords, with one or two flutes doubling the lead, is a very effective combination.

As mentioned earlier, trumpets and trombones are used quite frequently in Ska bands, with no saxophones. Salsa music sometimes uses trombone sections consisting of three or four trombones. A saxophone section can be useful as well, and will usually include one baritone sax, two tenors, and two altos.

What About Strings?

Arranging for strings is a very complicated process, and there are many books available on the subject. As most independent composers will not have easy access to string players, it has not been included in this text. Most string parts can be sequenced fairly easily for demo purposes, and an arranger can be hired by the producer to write string charts later, if need be.

Project 5.0: Compose a song with parts for horn section, or write horn parts for one of your existing compositions. Write out the parts in score format, untransposed, then copy the transposed parts from the score.

-- OR --

Transcribe the horn parts from a pop song (the song must be approved in advance by the instructor.) Write the parts in score format, and copy the transposed parts from the score.

(Source for this chapter: Lindsay, 1985)

Checklist of Assignments for Chapter 14

✓ **Written Assignment 14.1:** Transpose the melody for each instrument.

✓ **Written Assignment 14.2:** Harmonize notes in closed position, drop 2, drop 3, and drop 2 & 4.

✓ **Written Assignment 14.3:** Harmonize the 4-measure melody in the workbook.

✓ **Project 5.0:** Compose a song with parts for horn section, or write horn parts for one of your existing compositions.

✓ **-- OR --**

Transcribe the horn parts from a pop song, which include a horn section (the song must be approved in advance by the instructor.) Write the parts in score format, and copy the transposed parts from the score.

Brass and Woodwind Quick Reference: Range and Transposition

Instrument	Transposition	Range
Trumpet	Up a major 2nd	
Flugelhorn	Up a major 2nd	
Tenor Trombone	Nontransposed	
Bass Trombone	Nontransposed	
Soprano Saxophone	Up a major 2nd	
Alto Saxophone	Up a major 6th	
Tenor Saxophone	Up a major 9th	
Baritone Saxophone	Up a major 13th	
Flute	Nontransposed	

15

FINAL THOUGHTS

There are two types of composers in pop music today: 1.) Composer/Songwriter, Those who write for other people, and 2.) Artist/Composer, performing artists who write solely for themselves.

The composer/songwriter must stay hip to current musical styles. He or she often cannot afford to take chances musically, as this will affect the marketability of their songs. They must be musical "chameleons", able to compose convincingly in any and every musical genre.

Scoring for films can allow for artistic freedom, but there are still constraints. The music must fit the visual aspects and atmosphere of the film. Once the film composer has his or her "foot in the door", they can afford to forge a more personal artistic style. Some film directors will hire a composer with a unique artistic vision, because they believe that vision will fit their movie. Thus, in film music, there is a place for both the musical "chameleon" and the rugged individualist. This is, however, not true in most other realms of commercial music.

The artist/composer, however, ultimately has more freedom. However, there are many artist/composers whose style is so unique that they have never been signed to a major label. Thankfully, the Internet and the affordability of home studios and mass CD duplication seem to be leveling the field a bit. Today, it is much easier for the independent artist to distribute his or her music.

This is why many composers who wish to be musical innovators reluctantly become performing artists as well.

Popular Music as Art Music

There were several moments in the history of American Popular Music in which music for the masses and serious art music crossed a line. These met with varying degrees of success. One such moment was the early 1940's Bebop movement, when Charlie Parker, Dizzy Gillespie, Miles Davis, and others elevated the popular music of the day, jazz, into an art form. This was the beginning of the decline in popularity of jazz, which ultimately paved the way for Rock and Roll. Though jazz was still derided for many years by the artistic aristocracy, it is now respected by most as an art form.

This is not yet the case for the remainder of pop music; however, there is much disagreement in this area among critics and musicians alike. Some rock groups have come to enjoy at least a grudging respect from "serious" musicians and critics. Many of those who claimed that Rock was a passing fad have now realized that it is not (almost 50 years later.)

The fact that many colleges and universities are beginning to offer degrees in "commercial music" may be an indication that academia is taking pop music more seriously.

The first documented moment of ascension for Rock and Roll came in the mid-1960's, with the Beatles *Sgt. Pepper's Lonely Hearts Club Band* (as well as the Beach Boys *Pet Sounds*.) This did not signal the end of Rock and Roll as popular music, however. The Beatles continued their experimentation, but they still composed simple pop songs as well, maintaining their popularity to this day.

"Art Pop" music has continued to exist, but it has never achieved the level of popular success that the Beatles did. However, pop music has a tendency to continually reinvent itself. There is a constant trend of musical innovation followed by stagnation, followed by renewed innovation, etc. Often, the innovators are lost in the dust of the imitators when the major record labels snap them up in order to capitalize the newest trend.

The following is a brief list of examples of artistic and innovative movements in pop and rock music. Many of these innovators borrowed from elements of serious art music, and many others have borrowed only from other popular music styles.

Art/Progressive Rock

Bands like Yes, Genesis, Emerson Lake & Palmer, King Crimson, Velvet Underground, and many lesser-known artist/bands, made up the eclectic field that was termed as Art Rock or Progressive Rock. Many of these bands combined rock with elements of classical music and jazz. However, this was not always the case. Often, mixed meters, some orchestral sounds, and other elements borrowed from 20th Century classical music, such as *Musique Concrete* characterized the music.

David Bowie went through an Art Rock phase, and the Talking Heads were a late-1970's Art Rock band that enjoyed popularity in the 1980's with more simple pop songs.

Art and Progressive rock enjoyed brief popularity in the 1970's. It continues to exist to this day on the fringes of the mainstream.

Fusion

Much of the Art/Progressive Rock movement could also be placed in the Fusion category. In fact, today, any mixing of other genres with rock or pop is Fusion. However, in the late 1960's and the 1970's, the term Fusion described the fusion of jazz and rock. There were two fusion movements, one in jazz and one in rock. The jazz version of fusion began with the Miles Davis album *Bitches Brew*. Reportedly, Davis conceived the idea after hearing the music of Jimi Hendrix. He then put a band together with a group of young musicians, all of whom later came to dominate the Jazz Fusion scene of the 1970's. Some of the musicians who came out of Miles Davis fusion groups were: Herbie Hancock, Chick Corea, Joe Zawinul, John McLaughlin, and Wayne Shorter.

Jazz Fusion of this type was often characterized by the use of 7th and extended chords, more complex chord progressions and melodies, long improvisational sections, and mixed meters. Guitarists, such as John McLaughlin, used distortion, which was unheard-of in straight-ahead jazz. Randy Brecker, of the Brecker Brothers group, often used distortion and wah-wah pedals on his trumpet in his solos. McLaughlin's group, Mahavishnu Orchestra, also incorporated elements of classical music, with the use of strings.

Joe Zawinul and Wayne Shorter formed the band Weather Report in the 1970's. Weather Report had no guitarist. However, they discovered a young bassist named Jaco Pastorius, who revolutionized the playing of the electric bass, ripping the frets off his bass, and playing melodic bass lines.

Chicago and Blood, Sweat & Tears spearheaded the rock version of Fusion (sometimes called Jazz Rock). These were rock groups with added horn sections, and they were not as musically adventurous as their counterparts in Jazz were. They wrote pop songs with horn parts, adding a few 7th chords to make it sound "jazzier".

Jazz-rock died in the late-1970's. By this time, Blood, Sweat & Tears was gone, and Chicago had become a Top 40 band. Jazz Fusion evolved (or devolved) into Smooth Jazz, which has become the modern-day "elevator music". In fact, most of the great Jazz Fusion musicians of the 1970's moved into more straight-ahead jazz styles.

A modern form of Jazz Fusion is Acid Jazz, which blends elements of hip-hop, dance, and other styles with jazz. Exploration and musical innovation are still occurring in this style.

Improvisational/Aleatoric Music

Aleatoric, Indeterminate, or "Chance" music, is music that is open to the elements of chance. This can take many forms. In 20th century classical music, John Cage was the driving force in Aleatoric music. His work has influenced many areas of music, including popular music and jazz. Cage attempted to explore the boundaries of what is considered music. He borrowed many ideas from jazz, as they involved improvisational elements. Some of his works allowed the performer to work as a co-composer, improvising the music according to a few parameters.

Of course, improvisation has always been a component of all the musical styles that have evolved from the Afro-American musical tradition. Improvisation is much more prevalent (to varying degrees, depending on the style) in Jazz, but it is also present in the Blues, Rock, R&B, and other pop styles.

Use of the terms Improvisational or Aleatoric, in this case, would apply to music in which many of the elements are left to chance. The Free Jazz, or Avant-Garde Jazz, movement, which began in the early 1960's, was jazz in which none of the players had any written music. They just played what they felt. This could often be atonal and chaotic, depending on the abilities and ingenuity of the players.

Long improvisations characterize the live performances of "Jam Band" rock ensembles such as the Grateful Dead and Phish. These are rarely, if ever, atonal, because the bass player and drummer usually settle into patterns of repeated riffs, over which the other instrumentalists play. However, each performance will sound a bit different. That is perhaps why both of these band's concerts were usually sold out, even though their record sales were never huge. In this type of improvisational music, the band will often begin with a song they have written, launching into a long improvisational section in the middle or at the end. This is, of course, more similar to Bebop than Free Jazz, but it is rather unstructured compared to most Rock music.

The Beatles used Aleatoric elements in some of their work. For instance, the end of the song "Being for the Benefit of Mr. Kite" on *Sgt. Pepper* features a number of random circus and carnival sounds underneath the music. Reportedly, John Lennon and producer

George Martin recorded a variety of these sounds on tape. They then cut up the tapes, threw them in the air, and re-spliced them together in a random order. Thus, the selection of the sounds was determined ahead of time, but the order and combinations of those sounds were indeterminate.

Musique Concrete

Musique Concrete is another innovation of 20th Century classical music that made it's way into pop music. It is similar to sample-based composition in some ways. Early Musique Concrete composers, beginning in the late-1940's, would record non-musical sounds (called "Found Sounds," manipulate them in a variety of ways until they are almost unrecognizable, then combine them together, forming a new piece of "music." This was similar to (and most likely influenced by) the ideas of John Cage, exploring new ideas of what constitutes music. The Musique Concrete composers asserted that all sounds were music, whether they were natural sounds or sounds subject to electronic manipulation.

The Beatles used Musique Concrete in some of their musical experiments, most notable "Revolution No.9" on the *White Album*. The Electronic and Industrial Rock movements that began in the 1970's more whole-heartedly embraced the idea, however. Industrial Rock, in particular, is based on the use and manipulation of found sounds. These are usually combined with distorted guitars and vocals. Electronic Rock, which later became Techno, uses Musique Concrete elements much more sparingly. In general, the found sounds provide the rhythmic element in the music, and more traditional rock instruments such as guitar, bass and vocals, as well as traditional synthesizer sounds, provide the harmonic and melodic elements. There are exceptions, however.

Trent Reznor, better known as Nine Inch Nails, brought Industrial Rock into the mainstream in the early 1990's with a combination of melodic sensibility and industrial sounds. However, in his 1995 album *The Downward Spiral*, many of the songs were characterized by dense layers of manipulated found sounds, in addition to his characteristic melodies. Nevertheless, he achieved great commercial success with the album.

Early industrial bands were Throbbing Gristle and Einstanzer Neubaten, and Tangerine Dream and Kraftwerk were early techno/electronic pioneers.

Experimental Pop

Experimental describes music that is difficult to categorize. In fact, some use the terms Experimental and Eclectic interchangeably. However, Experimental bands will combine elements of Eclecticism, Musique Concrete, and Aleatoric Music with any number of styles or genres.

Wilco, an Alternative Country band, made an album of experimental rock in 2002, *Yankee Hotel Foxtrot*, that combined elements of Musique Concrete and Aleatoric music with a variety of rock and country sounds. Radiohead, beginning with their 1997 album *OK Computer*, have done a number of musical experiments combining Musique Concrete and other electronic sounds with their signature British sound. Both of these bands have achieved a measure of success with their experimental work.

Often, in these cases, the recording engineer and/or producer becomes an accomplice in the experimental and compositional process. This was certainly the case with George

Martin and the Beatles. Often, the process involves recording a song in a straightforward manner, and manipulating the arrangements and the musical sounds electronically. Thus, the compositional process cannot exist without the technological aspects of recording and sound production.

There are many bands that are far more experimental than Radiohead and Wilco, adding elements of atonality or chromaticism to the list of techniques they use.

Other Artistic Movements in Pop Music

Many popular music artists are beginning to fuse elements of pop with elements from other genres, especially Ethnic and World music. Typically, these bands and artists will use elements of three or more styles or genres, and they will often borrow from earlier musical styles. For instance, the band Supreme Beings of Leisure combines elements of Eastern music, Techno, Hip-hop, and 60's Rock, as well as others. The band Self combined elements of Grunge, Hip-hop, Techno, Jazz, 60's Rock, and many others.

Of course, this blending of genres has made its way into mainstream pop music to an extent. Many Hard Rock bands have embraced elements of Hip-Hop. Similarly, some Hard Rock and Hip-Hop music includes Eastern sounds. Rock influenced by Latin American and Caribbean music has enjoyed a resurge in popularity recently as well. Many dance and techno styles have elements of Reggae and Latin music. Various fusions of Country and Rock have been in existence for years, and modern Country music sounds quite a bit like Country Rock of the 1970's. It seems that artists and bands are beginning to realize that the limits of conventional pop music have been reached, and they are borrowing elements of other styles.

The above list of artistic trends in Popular Music is certainly not complete. There are large varieties of musical innovations that exist far out of the mainstream. Artists and groups that combine other artistic mediums with music are one example.

Future Trends in Pop Music

It is impossible to predict the future of Popular Music. As we have discussed, the current trend seems to be a continual combination of many different styles and compositional techniques. Some pop music is beginning to approach the point that classical music reached in the early part of the 20th Century, with the realization that we have reached the limits of traditional sounds and traditional tonality. However, it is highly doubtful that atonal rock music will ever catch on. One never knows, though.

Rock music has existed for around 50 years now. While the sound has changed quite a bit, there are still elements that have existed unchanged in all that time, such as the form of a pop song. 50 years from now, will popular music still sound essentially the same? Will it even exist anymore, or will it be replaced by something completely new? It can be argued that everything has already been done in pop music. Many of the "new" styles that crop up from time to time are just recycled versions of older styles.

Every artist or composer must find his or her artistic "voice". Musical innovation requires studying the music of those who came before you, learning their rules and conventions, and then finding creative ways to break those rules! This is not to say that all the rules must be broken; the discerning composer will decide which rules should be broken and which should not. It is up to the next generation of artists and composers to take popular music to new and innovative heights.

> **Project 6.0:** Compose a song of at least 2:30, any style, for rhythm section plus any other instruments. Try to incorporate as many elements you have learned in this text as possible, and pay special attention to the melody.

GLOSSARY

Aleatoric, Indeterminate, Chance Music: A 20th Century movement in Classical music, in which one or more musical elements are left to chance. Musicians often improvise much of the composition, making them, in effect, co-composers. The results of an Aleatoric composition such as *4'33''* by John Cage, where the performer sits on the stage for four minutes and 33 seconds without playing a note, is that the environmental sounds of the concert hall become the music. The Beatles used Aleatoric techniques in their experimental period, and many other jazz and pop artists have experimented with chance elements. In fact, one of the hallmarks of jazz is improvisation, which falls within this category.

Altered dominant chord: The Chord scale based on the seventh mode of melodic minor (Ionian $\sharp$1) in which all the extensions are sharped or flatted. The extensions are $\flat$9, $\sharp$9, $\sharp$11, and $\flat$13.

Altered extension: A chord extension that has been raised or lowered from its "natural" form. The natural form is that which is found in the major 7 chord: major 9th, perfect 11th, and major 13th.

Anticipation: A note that begins on a later subdivision of one beat (the second eighth-note or the fourth sixteenth-note) and continues into the next beat.

Asymmetric scale: A scale with an odd number of notes and unequal number of intervals between adjacent notes.

Atonal Music: Music in which the composer makes an effort to avoid any perception of tonality.

Augmentation: The statement of a theme in uniformly longer or shorter note-values, respectively than those originally associated with it.

Avoid tone or avoid note: The $\natural$11th of any chord that also contains a $\natural$3rd. Many jazz musicians consider the half-step clash between the $\natural$3rd and $\natural$11th undesirable.

Bar: A term used to describe a measure.

Bebop: The revolutionary style of jazz that evolved in the early 1940's, stressing scale-based improvisation.

Bird Blues: Charlie Parker's reharmonization of the blues.

Blue notes: Notes that are sung or played below the intended pitch, most commonly the third. Derived from the blues.

Blues: A 12-bar chord progression commonly found in jazz and other popular music styles.

Blues scale: A scale containing six notes, not including the octave. The minor form of the Pentatonic Scale with an added note. It contains two minor third intervals. The scale is derived from the blues.

Bridge: A major section of a song that often provides a musical contrast to the other sections and further clarifies the lyrical message. Typically, a bridge will seem to modulate to another key for at least a few measures, eventually leading to the original key or modulating to a new key for the next chorus. The bridge is usually placed near the end of the song, and often helped to build the musical and emotional intensity.

Cadence: A device used to bring music to a point of rest, or conclusion. Cadences are found in melodies as well as chord progressions. Typically the chord progression will cadence simultaneously with the melody.
Authentic Cadence: 5-1.
Plagal Cadence: 4-1.
Half Cadence: Any chord followed by the 5, for instance, 2m-5.
Deceptive Cadence: The 5 chord followed by any chord except 1, for example, 5-6m.

Chart: A printed or handwritten instrumental or vocal part for a composition. A chart can refer to a lead sheet; however, charts are also separate parts written for each individual instrument, which do not usually contain the melody. A chord chart is also sometimes called a chart, but charts often contain printed notes as well. A Nashville Numbering System arrangement is also called a chart.

Chord: A group of two or more notes sounded simultaneously.

Chord Changes, or "Changes": A term used to describe – 1. All of the chords in a song; 2. A chord progression; 3. The chord symbols notated on a chart, chord chart, or lead sheet.

Chord Chart: A notated arrangement of a song consisting only of the chord symbols and occasionally some rhythms, but no melody.

Chord nomenclature: The term used to describe the standard practice or system of chord symbol notation.

Chord progression: The term used to describe a series of chords that make up all or part of a musical composition. So named because the chords "progress" from one to the next.

Chord quality: The basic sound of a chord, i.e., minor, major, diminished or augmented, determined by the type of triad it contains, as well as the 7th.

Chord riff: A repeating series of chords, usually moving in parallel motion with a syncopated rhythm. A riff made up of chords (see *Riff*)

Chord scale: The scale or mode associated with a particular chord, and vice versa.

Chord substitutions: Used to replace or augment the standard chord changes, usually in areas of static harmony, in order to make the harmony more interesting. The most common form of chord substitution is the tritone substitution, but there are many other methods used.

Chord Suffix: A label following the pitch name of the chord, used to describe the *Chord Quality* (major, minor, diminished, augmented, sus.) Chord suffixes may also include the 7th, as well as any added extensions.

Chord symbol: A form of shorthand used to indicate the chords in a composition.

Chord-scale theory: The process of building a chord from the notes of a scale or mode.

Chorus: 1.) The section of a song that usually conveys the main message of the song. The chorus generally will consist of the same melody and lyrics every time. In addition, the chorus often contains the title of the song. 2.) The term used when playing or singing an improvised solo wherein the entire form of a composition is played one time through. Thus, if a soloist takes two choruses, they solo over the entire form twice.

Chromaticism: 1.) The use of all twelve notes found in the octave. 2.) The use of notes not found in the scale or mode on which a tonal composition is based. 3.) The term can also be used to describe a composition in which the tonal center is often shifting.

Chromatic Scale: A scale consisting of all twelve notes found in the octave.

Circle of Fifths: A graphic depiction of the relationship between the different major (and minor) keys. The key of C is usually at the 12 o'clock position, and if the circle is followed clockwise through the sharp keys, the next key is G, then D, A, E, and so on, each key being a 5th apart. Similarly, the flat keys proceed counter-clockwise from C in fifths: F, B♭, E♭, A♭.

Closed Position: A term used to describe chord voicings in which all of the chord tones are situated as close together as possible. In a closed position chord voicing, each voice is less than an octave away from any of the other voices.

Coda: The ending section of a song, after the last chorus. The coda may be a partial repeat of the chorus, a repeat of the introduction, or a repeat of the chorus with a fade-out. Also known as an *Outro*.

Diatonic Passing Chord: A passing chord in which all the notes conform to the key or chord scale.

Drop 2: A chord voicing in which the second voice from the top in a closed position chord is transposed down an octave, producing a more open voicing.

Drop 2 & 4: A chord voicing in which the second and fourth voices from the top in a 4-part closed position chord are transposed down an octave, producing a more open voicing.

Drop 3: A chord voicing in which the third voice from the top in a closed position chord is transposed down an octave, producing a more open voicing.

Elongation or Diminution: The practice in which a motive or theme is repeated using either longer or shorter note values.

Enharmonic Spelling: Pitches that sound the same but are named or "spelled" differently, such as C♯ and D♭.

Envelope: The attack, sustain, decay and release of a sound. A term borrowed from the science of acoustics.

Extensions: A chord tone which extends beyond the Root, 3rd, 5th and 7th, namely, the 9th, 11th or 13th.

Fake book: A book consisting of pared-down arrangements of songs in which only the melody, lyrics, and chord changes are provided, with no notated piano part. So named because the pianist, guitarist, or rhythm section is required to "fake" the accompaniment.

Falloff: The term used to describe a note that is sounded, followed by a downward glissando that tails off.

Fill: A short (no more than 2 measures) instrumental improvisation at the end of a phrase or section of a composition.

Graphic Analysis: A technique of melodic analysis, plotting lines on a graph to indicate the contour of a melody.

Groove: The rhythmic "feel" of a song, which can usually be identified by noting the amount of regularly-occurring syncopated rhythmic patterns and the strong beats in each measure. Most often defined by the drums as well as the bass. The term can also be used to describe how closely individual musicians are adhering to the rhythmic feel. For instance, a musician who is adhering to the rhythmic feel is often described as playing "in the groove".

Harmony: When two or more notes are sounded simultaneously.

Head: 1. The melody of a jazz standard; 2. In a jazz performance, the section of the song where the melody is played.

Interval: The distance between two notes.

Interlude: A short, usually instrumental, transitional section between major sections of a pop song, usually 4-8 measures. Also known as a *Transition*.

Introduction (Intro): An instrumental opening section of a song. Intros are usually shorter than the major sections of the song, and may contain material from the verse or chorus.

Inversion: The word used to describe a triad or 7th chord in which the bottom note is not the root.
> **First inversion:** The bottom note is the 3rd.
> **Second inversion:** The bottom note is the 5th.
> **Third inversion:** The bottom note is the 7th.

Inverted: An interval is inverted when the bottom note of the interval is transposed up an octave or the top note is transposed down an octave.

Jazz melodic minor scale: The ascending form of the melodic minor scale. A Major scale with a ♭3 or a Dorian scale with a raised 7th.

Lead sheet: A pared-down arrangement of a composition in which, only the melody, lyrics, and chord changes are provided, with no notated piano part.

Leading Tone: The 7th of a 5^7 chord, which descends or "leads" to the 3rd of the 1 chord by a half-step. The 3rd of a 5^7 chord also ascends to the root of the 1 chord by a half step. These leading tone relationships are in effect whenever there is chord movement of a fifth between a dominant 7 chord and a major 7 (or dominant 7) chord.

Melodic Riff: A repeating monophonic series of notes, similar to an ostinato in classical music.

Modal Jazz: A style of jazz in which the harmony lacks a traditional definition of tonal center, or 2-5-1 root movement.

Mode: A term derived from the ancient Greek word, which meant "mood". A mode can best be described as the notes of a scale played from any starting pitch within the scale. Thus, the first mode of a scale is the scale played in ascending form from the root to the octave above it. The second mode of a scale is found by playing the notes of the scale in ascending form from the second degree to the octave above it.

Motive: A musical statement of two or more notes, usually of short duration. Often a motive is thought to be the smallest recognizable component of a melody or theme. A motive is also considered a component of a musical phrase. For instance, a melody usually consists of two or more phrases, and a phrase usually consists of two or more motives.

Multi-Measure Rest: 1. A group of adjacent full-measure rests with a combined duration longer than two measures. 2. The symbol for a multi-measure rest, a long horizontal line with a vertical line on each end, with the number of measures centered directly above the horizontal line.

Musique Concrete: A movement in 20th Century Classical music that began in the late-1940's. Non-musical sounds, often from nature or city environments, were recorded and then electronically manipulated using a variety of techniques. This technique was embraced by the Beatles in their experimental period, and later by the Industrial Rock movement.

Nashville Numbering System: A notation system used in Nashville, as well as other parts of the country. It is similar to the Roman numeral system used for the analysis of Classical harmony; however, Arabic numbers are used instead. Chords are indicated by numbers, using standard chord suffixes. The 1 chord is the tonic of the key the song is in. Use of this system allows a song to be played in any key.

Nashville Number Charts: Arrangements that utilize the Nashville Numbering System.

Nontransposing Instruments: Instruments that are notated exactly as they sound.

Outro: See *Coda*

Outside the changes: Notes played or sung in an improvised solo that do not conform to the chord scales indicated in the chord progression.

Pad: A sustained chord, usually a half note or longer, played with little or no rhythmic syncopation. Pads can be played by almost any instrument or combination of instruments, but they are typically played by synthesizers, strings or horn section.

Parallel Passing Chord: A passing chord in which each voice approaches the next chord by the same interval.

Parent scales: The scale from which a mode is derived.

Pedal: A sustaining or repeating pitch in the bass with different chords played above it.

Phrase: A complete musical statement, often of relatively short duration. The term is borrowed from the study of spoken and written language. In language, a phrase is a smaller component of a sentence. Similarly, in music a phrase is a smaller component of a melody or theme. A phrase usually consists of a recognizable beginning, middle and end.

Phrygian Chord: The chord derived from the Phrygian mode, consisting of a major triad superimposed over a bass note 1/2 step below the root.

Pickup Note: When a melody or composition begins on a beat other than 1; usually beat 3 or 4 or a subdivision of one of those beats. Typically, when a song begins with a pickup note, there will be no rests before it. Instead, the first measure will be shortened to the length of the pickup note.

Polychord: One chord superimposed over another. In other words, a polychord is two (often unrelated) chords played at the same time.

Power Chord: A chord consisting of the root and 5th, with no 3rd. The root is usually doubled at the octave (sometimes even tripled at the octave above that) and the 5th may be doubled at the octave as well. This type of chord is most often played on guitar.

Pre-Chorus: The section of a song immediately preceding the chorus, usually after the verse. The pre-chorus typically occurs before almost every occurrence of the chorus, and it is often shorter than the other major sections of the song.

Quartal voicing: A method of voicing a chord by arranging the notes so that they are arranged or "stacked" a fourth apart.

Quintal voicing: A method of voicing a chord by arranging the notes so that they are arranged or "stacked" a fifth apart.

Real book: Another term used to describe a fake book consisting primarily of jazz compositions. The original Real Book was an illegal fake book (for which copyright permission had not been obtained) that was copied and distributed among jazz musicians for many years. At present, however, there are a number of legal, published jazz fake books that bear the title in some form.

Reharmonization, Reharm: Reharmonization is the process of using chord substitutions to alter the harmony of a composition. Arrangers will often reharmonize a song to make the arrangement unique. Composers sometimes reharmonize a pre-existing composition and compose a new melody. A composer's reharmonization of a song is also known as a Reharm (Bird blues is Charlie Parker's reharm of the blues chord progression.)

Retrograde: Reversing the note or interval order in a motive, so that the last note/interval is first, and the first note/interval is last.

Retrograde inversion: Reversing the interval order of a motive, and inverting each interval as well.

Rhythm changes: The chord changes to the famous Gershwin composition "I Got Rhythm". Many jazz compositions utilize this standard 32-bar chord progression.

Rhythm section: A group of instrumentalists, who provides rhythmic and harmonic support to an ensemble or soloist. The rhythm section consists of: (1) at least one percussion instrument, usually the drum set, (2) one bass instrument, usually the bass, and (3) at least one chordal or harmonic instrument, usually keyboard and/or guitar. The standard pop band is a rhythm section.

Riff: A repeating melodic or chordal pattern, often used as the basis for a composition. In cases where a song is not based on a riff, it may be used as a countermelody to the vocal line.

Root: The first note of a scale or chord scale.

Scale: A series of notes arranged in ascending or descending order.

Scalewise motion: The term used to describe a series of notes (in an improvised solo or a melody) separated by small intervals, usually half- or whole-steps. Conversely, a "leap" would be described as an interval of a minor third or larger.

Scoop: The process of initiating a note a minor or major 2nd below it and quickly sliding up to the pitch.

Secondary Dominant: A 5 chord borrowed from the key of the chord that follows it.

Sequence: A melodic motive that is repeated at a different pitch level. The motive can be performed the same at the new pitch level, or altered to fit the underlying chords.

7th Chord Tone Categories: A system used in harmonizing 7th chords to lead or melody notes. The categories are: Root, 3rd, 5th, and 7th. The arranger deduces which category the melody note belongs to, and fills in the harmony with notes from the remaining three categories.

Shake: The process of initiating a note, and then alternating it with a note a major 2nd or more above it, at least several times. A shake only works on notes with a value of a quarter note or longer. It is similar to the trill in classical music. On notes longer than a half-note, the note will sound for a moment, then the shake will begin, starting slow and speeding up as the end of the note nears. On shorter notes, the shake will commence as soon as the note is initiated. A shake is indicated with a wavy line above the note

Simile: A musical term placed in the measure immediately following a notated musical passage, indicating that the passage should continue to be played in the same manner, allowing the arranger to use only chord symbols and slash notation, rather than notate the passage again.

Slash Chords: One chord or triad superimposed over another chord, triad or root. A chord or triad over a root would be notated with a diagonal slash between the two elements, such as C7/B♭. A chord or triad over another chord or triad is arranged like a fraction, with the first chord on top and the second directly underneath, separated by a horizontal line, as in __C__.

B♭7

Spread Voicing: A chord voicing in which all of the voices are spaced in intervals that skip a chord tone between each voice. The voices in a spread voicing are always more than a 3rd apart, and the interval between the lowest and highest voice is more than an octave in chords of three or more parts.

Stabs: Short, percussive chords meant to accentuate the harmonies and groove. Usually played by brass, strings, or keyboards

Sus4: A chord with a suspended 4th in place of the 3rd.

Swing: A rhythmic style used in jazz. Swing is characterized by the placement of the two rhythmic subdivisions of the beat. At its most elemental, this subdivision can be described as a quarter note triplet followed by an eighth-note triplet, rather than two successive eighth-notes. However, throughout the evolution of jazz, the rhythmic placement of the second subdivision has changed (see Swing Feel.)

Swing Era: Jazz of the 1930's.

Symmetric Scale: A scale with an even number of notes and an equal number of intervals between adjacent notes.

Syncopation: Placing an accent upon a normally unaccented part of the beat or measure.

Synthetic scales: Non-standard scales consisting of varied combinations of intervals between scale degrees. Synthetic scales can be constructed in a number of ways, including combining the notes of two or more triads or chords, varying the standard order of half- and whole-steps, and adding a note to an existing scale.

Tessitura: A specific region of the range of a voice or instrument. The range of a voice or instrument is the area from the lowest possible note to the highest possible note. The term tessitura is used to describe any smaller area within that range.

Tetrachords: A grouping of four notes played individually in succession. The term, from the Latin root Tetra, meaning three, describes the three intervals contained between the four notes. The intervals are usually seconds.

Theme: A musical idea or melodic statement, often recognizable or memorable. Like a phrase, this can be a component of a melody, or a complete melody upon which a composition is based.

Tin Pan Alley: An area in New York in the early 20th Century that housed many popular music publishing companies.

Time Feel: The way in which a performer functions within the rhythmic confines of the style.

Tonality: The organization of musical material around a central note, usually called the *Tonic* or *Tonal Center*. Tonality most often refers to music composed in the traditional major or minor keys. However, modal music is often perceived as tonal.

Tonal Music: Music that is organized around a certain tonic note or tonal center. Most Classical music prior to the 20th century was tonal in nature. Much popular music is also tonal, although most modern composers do not adhere to the strict traditional rules of tonality.

Tonic, Tonal Center: The central note around which tonal music is organized. In the major scale, for instance, the tonic is the root or first note of the scale.

Transcription: As used in the text, this term refers to the process of learning to play or sing, or writing out by ear, the notes of a recorded performance.

Transition: See *Interlude*.

Transposing Instruments: Instruments for which the notated pitch is different than the actual pitch sounded.

Triad: A group of three notes sounded simultaneously, usually separated by thirds.

Tritone Substitution or Tritone Sub: The practice of replacing a dominant 7 chord with another dominant 7 chord a tritone away. This practice is useful because every dominant 7 chord shares a 3rd and 7th with another dominant 7 chord a tritone apart. One of the most common types of chord substitutions.

Turnaround: A pivot chord or chords usually designed to facilitate a return to the beginning of a song or repeated section (usually a 2-5 or 1-6-2-5 progression.)

2-5-1: Subdominant-dominant-tonic chord progression. The term originated in the study of traditional music theory and harmony. This type of progression is generally considered to establish a tonal center. The 2 chord is minor (or half-diminished,) the 5 chord is a dominant 7, and the 1 chord is a major triad, major 6 or major 7 chord. A very common chord progression in standard jazz compositions.

Upper-structure, upper-structure triads: The "upper" component of a jazz chord, consisting usually of the extensions and occasionally the seventh. As the extensions (and the seventh) are each a third apart, they can be thought of as a chord residing over another chord. The upper-structure usually does not include the primary chord tones, i.e., root, third, and fifth; However, the melodic minor augmented-major 7 upper-structure encompasses primary chord tones in some of the chord scales, such as the Ionian ♯1 mode.

Vamp: A chord progression or short section of a song that is repeated many times. The number of repeats is left to the performers.

Verse: 1.) The major section of a song that usually occurs first, after the introduction. A verse is usually made up of the same melody, but with different lyrics each time. 2.) In many jazz standards, the introductory section. It is similar to a recitative in opera, as it is often sung or played freely, with no steady tempo.

Voicing: An arrangement of the notes or "voices" of a chord, usually for piano or guitar, as well as instrumental ensembles.

Walking bass: A style of bass playing used in swing-based jazz. A note is played on every beat of the measure, and notes are usually arranged scalewise, although at times chord tones are arpeggiated. This style is so named because the bassist is usually "walking" up or down a scale.

CHORD VOICINGS FOR GUITAR

The following are some suggested guitar voicings for some of the chords used in the text. Some of these have been introduced earlier in the text, but they are included here anyway. It is assumed that most guitarists will know all of the major and minor triadic chord voicings. For slash chord voicings, refer to chapter 5.

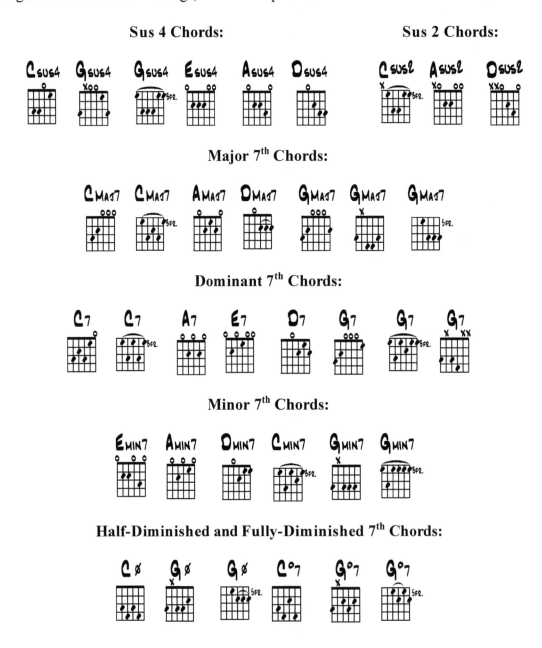

Dominant and Major 7th #5 Chords:

Minor-Major 7th Chords:

Dominant 7th Sus4 Chords:

6th Chords:

6/9 Chords:

9th Chords:

11th and 13th Chords:

9th and 13th Sus4 Chords:

Major 7th #11 Chords:

Dominant 7th #11 Chords:

Altered Dominant 7th Chords:

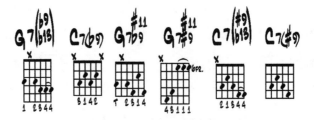

215

REFERENCES

Bruce, Dix. 2000. *Guide to the Capo, Transposing, and the Nashville Numbering System.* Pacific, MO: Mel Bay Publications, Inc.

Jones, George Thaddeus. 1974. *Music Theory.* New York: HarperCollins Publishers, Inc.

Levine, Mark. 1995. *The Jazz Theory Book.* Petaluma, CA: Sher Music Co.

Lindsay, Gary. 1985. *Modern Arranging.* Miami, FL.: by the author.

Lindsay, Gary. 1985. *Modern Arranging II.* Miami, FL.: by the author.

Randel, Don Michael, ed. 1969. *The New Harvard Dictionary of Music.* Cambridge, MA: Harvard University Press.

Slonimsky, Nicolas. 1986. *Thesaurus of scales and melodic patterns.* New York: Schirmer Books. Original edition, New York: C. Scribner, 1947.